Lonely planet

Pocket

HONOLULU

TOP SIGHTS • LOCAL LIFE • MADE EASY

D0974711

Craig McLachlan

In This Book

QuickStart Guide

Your keys to under-standing the city – we help you decide what to do and how to do it

Need to Know
Tips for a smooth trip

Neighborhoods
What's where

Explore Honolulu

The best things to see and do, neighborhood by neighborhood

Top Sights
Make the most of your visit

Local Life
The insider's city

The Best of Honolulu

The city's highlights in handy lists to help you plan

Best Walks
See the city on foot

Honolulu' Best...
The best experiences

Survival Guide

Tips and tricks for a seamless, hassle-free city experience

Getting Around
Travel like a local

Essential Information
Including where to stay

Our selection of the city's best places to eat, drink and experience:

⊙ **Sights**

❌ **Eating**

🄟 **Drinking**

✪ **Entertainment**

🄐 **Shopping**

These symbols give you the vital information for each listing:

📞 Telephone Numbers	🄵 Family-Friendly
⊙ Opening Hours	🐾 Pet-Friendly
🄿 Parking	🚌 Bus
⊖ Nonsmoking	⛴ Ferry
@ Internet Access	Ⓜ Metro
📶 Wi-Fi Access	Ⓢ Subway
🍃 Vegetarian Selection	🄣 Tram
🄐 English-Language Menu	🚃 Train

Find each listing quickly on maps for each neighborhood:

Bar Hemingway

16 🄟 Map p233, B2

Legend has it that Hem self, wielding a machine rate this timber-pan ered bar during showpiece is a en by Papa ar town. Dress s.com; Hôtel Rit ⊙6.30pm-2a

16 🄟

6 ⊙ Plac

Lonely Planet's Honolulu

Lonely Planet Pocket Guides are designed to get you straight to the heart of the city.

Inside you'll find all the must-see sights, plus tips to make your visit to each one really memorable. We've split the city into easy-to-navigate neighborhoods and provided clear maps so you'll find your way around with ease. Our expert authors have searched out the best of the city: walks, food, nightlife and shopping, to name a few. Because you want to explore, our 'Local Life' pages will take you to some of the most exciting areas to experience the real Honolulu.

And of course you'll find all the practical tips you need for a smooth trip: itineraries for short visits, how to get around, and how much to tip the guy who serves you a drink at the end of a long day's exploration. It's your guarantee of a really great experience.

Our Promise

You can trust our travel information because Lonely Planet authors visit the places we write about, each and every edition. We never accept freebies for positive coverage, so you can rely on us to tell it like it is.

QuickStart Guide 7

Explore Honolulu 21

Worth a Trip:

QuickStart Guide

Welcome to Honolulu

Landing at Honolulu's airport may plunge you into the Hawaiian-style urban jungle, but relax, it's still Polynesia. Even among downtown high-rises, you'll find capital city power brokers in breezy aloha shirts. By day, inspect royal feathered capes or hang out at the beach, then swizzle mai tais while slack key guitars play at Waikiki Beach after dark.

Waikiki Beach (p76)
DHOXAX / SHUTTERSTOCK ©

Honolulu
Top Sights

Kuhio Beach (p70)

Kuhio Beach in Waikiki has everything on offer from protected swimming to surfing lessons, outrigger-canoe rides to catamaran trips, and even a free sunset-hula and Hawaiian music show.

'Iolani Palace (p24)

'Iolani Palace, the USA's only royal palace, has been lovingly and painstakingly renovated. No other place evokes a more poignant sense of Hawaii's history.

Hanauma Bay
(p106)

This wide, curved bay of sapphire and turquoise waters protected by a coral reef is a gem, especially for snorkelers. Head here to eyeball technicolor tropical fish through your mask.

Pearl Harbor
(p64)

One of the USA's most significant WWII sites, the WWII Valor in the Pacific National Monument at Pearl Harbor narrates the history of the attack and commemorates fallen service members.

Diamond Head
(p96)

A dramatic backdrop for Waikiki Beach, Diamond Head is one of the best-known landmarks in Hawaii. It was named in 1825 when British sailors thought they'd found diamonds and struck it rich.

Honolulu Museum of Art (p46)

The three campuses of this exceptional fine arts museum may be the most pleasant surprise of your trip to Hawaii. Inviting and airy with stunning exhibitions and collections.

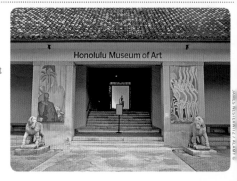

Honolulu Museum of Art

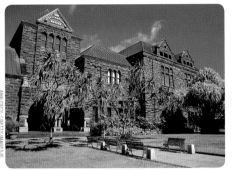

Bishop Museum
(p60)

One of the finest Polynesian anthropological museums in the world, Bishop Museum is considered to be Honolulu's version of the Smithsonian Institute. An attraction for the whole family.

Shangri La (p98)

Celebrity Doris Duke's passion for both Hawaii and Islamic art is encapsulated at Shangri La, her seasonal residence on Black Point, in the shadow of Diamond Head.

Lyon Arboretum & Upper Manoa Valley
(p62)

O'ahu is not all surf and sand. Inland are lush, verdant mountains and valleys, hiking trails and botanical gardens. Make the most of the green and explore the Upper Manoa Valley.

Honolulu
Local Life

Insider tips to help you find the real city

After checking off Honolulu's top sights, here's how you can experience what makes the city tick – hip local hangouts, neighborhood favorites, family hotspots and quirky shops that make up multiethnic Honolulu.

Historic Chinatown Walk (p26)

▶ Multiethnic hotspots
▶ Honolulu history

Though most Chinese entrepreneurs have long since moved out and been replaced by newer immigrants, the scent of burning incense still wafts through Chinatown's buzzing markets, fire-breathing dragons spiral up the columns of buildings and steaming dim sum awakens even the sleepiest of appetites.

Hang Out in Ala Moana (p48)

▶ Beach options
▶ Shopping spots

Locals know that Ala Moana offers more than just a shopping center.

Ward Center and Ward Warehouse offer excellent eating and browsing options, while the beach park and Magic Island are stunners that many staying in Waikiki don't even realize are there.

Stroll Like a UH Student (p58)

▶ Student days
▶ Drinking options

The main campus of the University of Hawai'i is breezy, tree-shaded and crowded with students from the mainland, Hawaii itself and countries all around the world. The UH campus and surrounding areas feel youthful, with a collection of cafes, eclectic restaurants and one-of-a-kind shops.

A Wander Through Waikiki (p72)

▶ Relaxed Waikiki
▶ Beaches and parks

Waikiki may be full of tourists, but don't forget that the locals live here too. From the southern end of Kuhio Beach Park, avenues radiate off in different directions to local spots like Kaimana Beach, Waikiki School (lucky kids!) and Waikiki-Kapahulu Library.

Kalapawai Market (p122)

Volleyball players, Ala Moana Beach Park (p49)

Other great places to experience the city like a local:

Gyotaku by Naoki (p118)

Fresh Cafe Downtown (p34)

Kalapawai Market (p122)

Tin Can Mailman (p42)

Waikiki Community Center (p79)

Waiola Shave Ice (p86)

People's Open Market (p85)

KCC Farmers Market (p102)

Tamura's Poke (p103)

Honolulu
Day Planner

Day One

☀ Get an early start and head to Honolulu's historical district. **'Iolani Palace** (p24), the **State Capitol** (p30) and the **Hawai'i State Art Museum** (p30) are due some of your limited time. Take a break at **Cafe Julia** (p126) before walking through downtown to check out the views from **Aloha Tower** (p33).

☀ You're going to Waikiki this afternoon. Spend an hour or two at **Kuhio Beach Park** (p70) with some quality sand and water time. Don't miss the **Duke Kahanamoku Statue** (p89) and consider a **Na Hoku II Catamaran** (p78) cruise.

☽ Watch the free **Kuhio Beach Torch Lighting & Hula Show** (p71), then head in for drinks at **House Without a Key** (p88). **Roy's Waikiki** (p83) is a great option for dinner and the Royal Hawaiian Hotel's low-key **Mai Tai Bar** (p88) for after.

Day Two

☀ It's going to be a busy day so get a good start. Head to **WWII Valor in the Pacific National Monument** (p65) at Pearl Harbor, but keep your time constraints in mind. At the least, you'll want to head out to the **USS Arizona Memorial** (p65) and **Battleship Missouri Memorial** (p65).

☀ If you can manage it, get to **Helena's Hawaiian Food** (p133) for lunch. It's few blocks from **Bishop Museum** (p61), where you'll be heading next. The **Hawaiian Hall** is stunning and everyone enjoys the **Science Adventure Center**.

☽ On your way home, drop into **Uncle Bo's Pupu Bar & Grill** (p133) on Kapahulu Ave, inland from the main Waikiki strip. You'll need to go to **Leonard's** (p133), a bit further up the road, for *malasadas* (Portuguese-style doughnuts) for dessert. If you're still going, have a drink at **RumFire** (p84) at the Sheraton Waikiki.

Short on time?
We've arranged Honolulu's must-sees into these day-by-day itineraries to make sure you see the very best of the city in the time you have available.

Day Three

☀ You're in for an early morning to climb **Diamond Head** (p96) before the crowds and heat of the day hit. Drop in to **Diamond Head Cove Health Bar** (p73) either on the way or way back for refreshments. You'll need a swim at **Sans Souci Beach** (p78) to get you ready for the rest of the day.

☀ Head to the **Honolulu Museum of Art** (p47) and peruse this exceptional fine arts museum, timing your visit with a tour to **Shangri La** (p98) – all tours to Doris Duke's former residence depart from the museum. The **Honolulu Museum of Art Cafe** (p54) is a great spot for lunch.

☾ Later in the afternoon, carry on from there into Chinatown where dinner at **The Pig & the Lady** (p37) can be followed up by some jazz or blues at **Dragon Upstairs** (p40), an intimate spot directly above **Hank's Cafe** (p39). There's plenty going on in Chinatown if you're into bar-hopping.

Day Four

☀ Start your day early and get out to **Hanauma Bay** (p106) for some quality snorkeling before the crowds arrive. **Kokonuts Shave Ice & Snacks** (p111) and **Bubbies** (p111) are in Hawai'i Kai's **Koko Marina Center** to quench your need for refreshments.

☀ Take time out for stops at **Lana'i Lookout** (p109), **Halona Blowhole** (p109) and **Sandy Beach Park** (p109) before rounding the island's easternmost point at **Makapu'u Point**. Drive into **Waimanalo Bay Beach Park** (p116) for a quick swim or a stroll on the beach, followed by sustenance at **Sweet Home Waimanalo** (p120). Head up to Kane'ohe and drop in to **Gyotaku by Naoki** (p118) before visiting the **Valley of the Temples & Byōdō-In** (p117).

☾ **Kailua Beach** (p116) awaits for a late afternoon stroll, followed by some shopping at the **Kailua Shopping Center** (p123) and a relaxed dinner at **Kailua Town Pub & Grill** (p122). Don't have too many drinks though: you'll need to drive back over the Pali Hwy to Honolulu or Waikiki.

Need to Know

For more information,
see Survival Guide (p146)

Currency
US dollar ($)

Language
English, Hawaiian

Visas
Generally not required for stays of 90 days
or less for citizens of Visa Waiver Program
(VWP) countries with ESTA approval.

Money
ATMs widely available. Credit cards widely
accepted; often required for reservations.

Cell Phones
International travelers need a multiband
GSM phone; SIM cards are widely available.
US carrier Verizon has the best network.

Time
Hawaii-Aleutian Standard Time (GMT/UTC
minus 10 hours); no daylight saving.

Plugs & Adaptors
Plugs are the same as on the US mainland,
for the most part using
two flat pins; current is 120V.

Tipping
Tipping practices are the same as on the US
mainland – 15% to 20% at
restaurants and bars.

❶ Before You Go

Your Daily Budget

Budget less than $150
▸ Waikiki hostel: $25–$35
▸ Walk to the beach
▸ Buses and a taxi or two to get around
▸ Mostly self-catering and plate lunches

Midrange $150–$350
▸ Waikiki budget hotel or Kailua vacation
rental: $90–$160
▸ Car rental for a couple of days
▸ Activities like surfing or stand-up paddling
▸ Restaurant meals as well as food-truck fare

Top End over $350
▸ Full-service resort room
▸ Top chef-made meals
▸ Whale-watching tours, activity rentals, spa
services

Useful Websites
▸ **Lonely Planet** (www.lonelyplanet.com)
Destination information, hotel bookings,
traveler forum and more.

▸ **Hawaii Visitors and Convention Bureau**
(www.gohawaii.com) Official tourism site;
comprehensive events calendar.

▸ **Honolulu Star-Advertiser** (www.
staradvertiser.com) Hawaii's biggest daily
newspaper.

Advance Planning
▸ **Two weeks before** Reserve in-demand
activities such as Valor in the Pacific
National Monument, 'Iolani Palace and
Doris Duke's Shangri La.

▸ **One week before** Make reservations for
any top restaurants, especially in Waikiki
and Honolulu.

② Arriving in Honolulu

Honolulu International Airport (HNL; http://hawaii.gov/hnl) The vast majority of flights into Hawaii land here, about 6 miles northwest of downtown Honolulu and 9 miles northwest of Waikiki. O'ahu's only commercial airport, it's a hub for domestic, international and inter-island flights.

✈ From Honolulu International Airport

Airport shuttle one-way/round-trip $15/30 to Waikiki; operates 24 hours (every 20 to 60 minutes).

Taxi Metered, $35 to $45 to Waikiki, 20 to 45 minutes depending on traffic.

Car Via Hwy 92 (Nimitz Fwy/Ala Moana Blvd) or H-1 (Lunalilo) Fwy to Waikiki.

Bus Routes 19 and 20 to Waikiki (one carry-on bag only per person) $2.50, every 20 to 60 minutes from 6am to 11pm daily.

✈ At the Airport

The airport is a modern facility with all the usual amenities such as currency exchange booths, duty-free shops and fast-food eateries, as well as flower-lei stands. You'll find visitor information desks, car-rental counters and courtesy phones in the baggage claim area.

③ Getting Around

O'ahu and Honolulu's only public transportation is TheBus, an extensive network that is convenient and easy to use, but you can't set your watch by it. A rental car is a good option unless you are planning to just stay in Waikiki.

🚌 Bus

TheBus (www.thebus.org) is a good way to get around if you have time on your side; schedules are frequent, service is reliable and fares are inexpensive.

🚗 Car

Most visitors on O'ahu rent their own vehicles; this is without doubt the easiest way to get around. Parking charges are high in Waikiki; it may pay to hire a car by the day from a Waikiki rental outlet rather than hiring a car from the airport for your entire stay.

🚲 Bicycle

Cycling around O'ahu is a great, nonpolluting way to travel, but realistically, as a primary mode of transportation, cycling can be challenge.

Moped & Motorcycle

Surprisingly, a moped or motorcycle can be more expensive to rent than a car. Both are rented in Waikiki, but you'll have to contend with heavy urban traffic.

🚗 Taxi

Taxis are metered and readily available at the airport, resort hotels and shopping malls, but otherwise you'll probably need to call for one.

Honolulu
Neighborhoods

Downtown Honolulu & Chinatown (p22)
Explore Hawaii's boisterous capital – the historic district, the high-rises of Downtown and the old and the modern in Chinatown.

◉ Top Sights
'Iolani Palace

Diamond Head & Kahala (p94)
Climb incomparable Diamond Head, visit Doris Duke's former mansion, Shangri La, and cruise the wealthy suburb of Kahala.

◉ Top Sights
Diamond Head
Shangri La

Ala Moana & Around (p44)
Enjoy sand and sea at Ala Moana Beach Park before visiting the world's largest open-air shopping center

◉ Top Sights
Honolulu Museum of Art

Waikiki (p68)
Hit the water, laze in the sun, try your hand at surfing and then sip cocktails as the sun sets.

◉ Top Sights
Kuhio Beach

'Iolani Palace ◉

Honolulu Museum of Art ◉

Kuhio Beach ◉

Diamond Head ◉

Shangri La ◉

Kailua & Kane'ohe (p112)

Kailua is a great base to relax and explore the turquoise bays, white-sand beaches and lush vegetation of the quieter side of the island.

Worth a Trip
◉ Top Sights

Bishop Museum

Lyon Arboretum & Upper Manoa Valley

Pearl Harbor

Hawai'i Kai & Southeast O'ahu (p104)

Snorkeling at its best at Hanauma Bay, plus watersports, hiking and sightseeing hotspots galore.

◉ Top Sights

Hanauma Bay

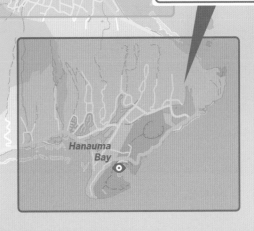

Hanauma Bay

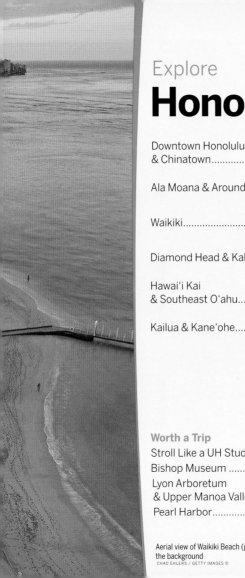

Explore
Honolulu

Worth a Trip

Aerial view of Waikiki Beach (p76), with Diamond Head (p96) in
the background
CHAD EHLERS / GETTY IMAGES ©

Explore

Downtown Honolulu & Chinatown

Here in Honolulu, you get to shake hands with the real Hawaii.
A boisterous Polynesian capital, Honolulu delivers an island-style
mixed plate of experiences. In Downtown you'll find an unmatched
collection of historic sites, museums and gardens – including the
USA's only royal palace – while in Chinatown you can poke your way
around intriguing alleyways, eateries and marketplaces.

The Sights in a Day

 Start your day with a walk around the **National Memorial Cemetery of the Pacific** (p33), known locally as the Punchbowl. Next up, head to Downtown. You'll be on your feet from here. Visit **ʻIolani Palace** (p24), then head over Richards St to **Cafe Julia** (p38) for lunch.

Wander up Richards to the thought-provoking **Hawaiʻi State Art Museum** (p30). Next, walk down past the **Father Damien Statue** (p30), through the center of the **State Capitol** (p30), past the **Queen Liliʻuokalani Statue** (p25), and through the **ʻIolani Palace** (p24) grounds to Aliʻiolani Hale with its **Kamehameha the Great Statue** (p31) out front.

It's time to walk northwest on King St to Chinatown. Take a break at **Vita Juice** (p34) in Fort Street Mall, then check out the beautifully re-stored **Hawaii Theatre** (p27). Wander the atmospheric streets. Dinner at **The Pig & the Lady** (p37) is a great option, then head to **Dragon Upstairs** (p40) for some soothing jazz.

For a local's day in Chinatown, see p26.

 Top Sights
ʻIolani Palace (p24)

 Local Life
Historic Chinatown (p26)

 Best of Honolulu

Eating
Cafe Julia (p38)

The Pig & the Lady (p37)

Drinking & Entertainment
Dragon Upstairs (p40)

Hawaii Theatre (p27)

Kumu Kahua Theatre (p42)

Museums
ʻIolani Palace (p24)

Mission Houses Museum (p32)

Hawaiʻi State Art Museum (p30)

Gardens, Sanctuaries & Cemeteries
Foster Botanical Garden (p33)

National Memorial Cemetery of the Pacific (p33)

Getting There

🚌 **Bus** 2, 4, 8, 13, 19, 20 & 42

🚗 **Car** The H-1 (Lunalilo Fwy) has a number of downtown exits. Hwy 92 (Ala Moana Blvd/Nimitz Hwy) is also close by. There are a number of one-way streets. There is metered parking plus municipal parking lots and garages.

Top Sights
'Iolani Palace

Perhaps no other place evokes a more poignant sense of Hawaii's history than this royal palace where plots and counter-plots simmered. Commissioned by King David Kalakaua (r 1874–91) and completed in 1882, the palace did little to assert Hawaii's sovereignty over powerful US-influenced business interests, who overthrew the kingdom in 1893. The palace then served as the capitol of the republic, then the territory and later the state of Hawaii. The building has been painstakingly restored to its former glory.

Map p28, D5

info 808-538-1471, tour reservations 808-522-0832

www.iolanipalace.org

364 S King St

grounds admission free, adult/child basement galleries $7/3, self-guided audiotour $15/6, guided tour $22/6

9am-5pm Mon-Sat

'Iolani Palace at dusk

Don't Miss

The Coronation Pavilion

Keli'iponi Hale, the Coronation Pavilion, was
built for the 1883 coronation of King David
Kalakaua and Queen Kapi'olani. Often used for
the inauguration of Governors of the State of
Hawaii, this Victorian-style gazebo is on the
western lawn of the palace grounds.

'Iolani Barracks

Presently housing the palace ticket office, shop
and video theater, the impressive 'Iolani Barracks
was built of coral blocks and completed in 1871
on the site of the present state capitol. After the
overthrow of the Hawaiian monarchy and the
disbanding of the Royal Guard, the building had
various uses until it was dismantled block by
block and reconstructed at its present site just to
the north of the palace in 1965.

Queen Lili'uokalani Statue

Pointedly positioned between the state capitol
building and 'Iolani Palace is a life-size bronze
statue of Queen Lili'uokalani, Hawaii's last reigning monarch. She holds a copy of the Hawaiian
constitution she wrote in 1893 in an attempt to
strengthen Hawaiian rule; 'Aloha 'Oe,' a popular
song she composed; and *Kumulipo*, the traditional Hawaiian chant of creation.

Royal Hawaiian Band Concerts

With a long tradition of sharing Hawaii's music
with the world, the Royal Hawaiian Band pre-
sents free concerts on the 'Iolani Palace Grounds
most Fridays (check the schedule online), from
noon to 1pm, weather permitting.

☑ Top Tips

▶ It's advisable to call
ahead for reservations
and to double-check
schedules, especially
during busy periods.

▶ If you're short on time
or the tours are sold
out, head downstairs to
the basement's gallery
exhibits, which include
royal regalia, historical
photographs and recon-
structions of the palace
kitchen and chamber-
lain's office.

▶ *Kapu* means 'forbid-
den', but more important-
ly, it also means 'sacred'
or 'consecrated.' Respect
the sanctity of the Palace
grounds and anywhere
marked *kapu*.

✕ Take a Break

Cross over Richards
St to the charming old
YMCA Laniakea building
and quench your thirst
or hunger pains at Cafe
Julia (p38).

Local Life
Historic Chinatown Walk

Though most successful Chinese entrepreneurs have long since moved out, making room for newer waves of mainly Southeast Asian immigrants, the scent of burning incense still wafts through Chinatown's buzzing markets, fire-breathing dragons spiral up the columns of buildings and steaming dim sum awakens even the sleepiest of appetites. Take a few hours to enjoy a wander through Honolulu's historic Chinatown.

❶ The Stone Lions

Start at the stone lions flanking Hotel St at **Dr Sun Yat-sen Memorial Park**. Sun Yat-sen lived in Hawaii from 1879, was educated at 'Iolani School and O'ahu College (later to become Punahou School), and became President of the Republic of China in 1912. Check out the park's **statue of the flying turtle** (*honu*) over the pond.

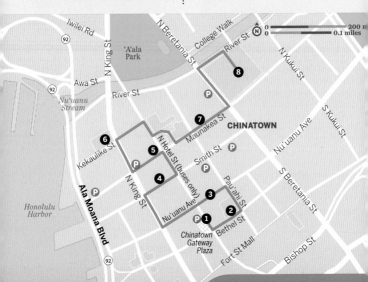

❷ Hawaii Theatre

Just up Bethel St and beautifully restored, the **Hawaii Theatre** (☎808-528-0506; www.hawaiitheatre.com; 1130 Bethel St) is the grande dame of O'ahu's theater scene, a major venue for dance, music and theater. Nicknamed the 'Pride of the Pacific', it hosts top Hawaii musicians, contemporary plays, international touring acts and film festivals.

❸ Nu'uanu Ave

Sailors used to hang out and drink along Nu'uanu. The avenue's granite-block sidewalks are themselves relics, the discarded ballast of 19th-century trading ships. At the corner of King St, peek into the **First Hawaiian Bank** with its antique wooden teller cages that had a cameo in the TV show *Lost*.

❹ Hawai'i Heritage Center

The community-run **Hawai'i Heritage Center** is a friendly gallery that displays historical and cultural exhibitions about O'ahu's Chinese, Japanese and other ethnic communities – including the Scots! Turn left onto seedy **Hotel St**, historically Honolulu's red-light district and now a row of trendy lounges, nightclubs, eateries and coffeehouses.

❺ Wo Fat Building

At the corner of Maunakea St, opposite the Chinatown Police Station, the ornate facade of the **Wo Fat Building** resembles a Chinese temple. The building – and, incidentally, also the villain of the *Hawaii Five-0* TV series – is named after Honolulu's oldest restaurant, which opened here in 1882 (it's now closed).

❻ Chinatown Markets

On King St, continue past the red pillars coiled with dragons outside the **Bank of Hawaii** to the corner of Kekaulike St and venture inside the buzzing **O'ahu Market**. In the pedestrian mall opposite is the newer, but equally vibrant, **Kekaulike Market**, while the **Maunakea Marketplace**, off Hotel St, has an intriguing and popular food court.

❼ Lei Shops & Herbalists

Back on Maunakea and heading northeast, you'll pass **lei shops** where skilled artisans string and braid blossom after blossom, filling the air with the scent of *pikake*. Keep your eye open for **herbalists** and **acupuncturists**. Cross S Beretania St, then head left down to the riverside.

❽ Chinatown Cultural Plaza

A **statue of Dr Sun Yat-sen** stands guard over the senior citizens playing checkers and cards at stone tables outdoors at the River St pedestrian mall. End your stroll by taking a break at one of the countless Chinese restaurants in the sprawling multistory **Chinatown Cultural Plaza**.

School St

Lunalilo Fwy

Pali Hwy

61

98

12

Vineyard St

Vineyard St

Queen Emma Sq

Cathedral of St Andrew

9

Queen Emma St

Washington Place

8

Foster Botanical Garden

11

N Vineyard Blvd

S Kukui St

S Beretania St

Hawai'i State Art Museum

98

Nu'uanu Ave

N Kukui St

S Beretania St

S Beretania St

Maunakea St

River St

CHINATOWN

Bethel St

S Hotel St

Union Mall

DOWNTOWN

35

33

19

39

23

16

15

17

Beretania Park

College Walk

26

Nu'uanu Ave

27

Chinatown Gateway Plaza

28

Fort St Mall

'A'ala St

N Beretania St

Pau'ahi St

25 22

21

31

S King St

36

'A'ala Park

River St

N Hotel St (buses only)

32 34 30

S King St

18 20

37

N King St

24

Maunakea St

N King St

Smith St

S Auahi St

92

Awa St

Ke'eaumoku St

Nu'uanu Stream

Ala Moana Blvd

92

Iwilei Rd

92

Honolulu Harbor

200 m
0.1 miles

Father
Damien ⊙2
Statue
⊙1
State
Capitol

'Iolani
Palace

⊙ Likelike St

Richards St

S King St

Hawaiian Mission
Houses Historic
Site and Archives

Kawaiaha'o St

⊙7

KAKA'AKO

South St

Kawaiaha'o
Church

Historic
Cemetery

6 ⊙

Cemetery

Punchbowl St

S King St

5 ⊙ Kamehameha
4 ⊙⊙ the Great
Ali'iolani Hale Statue

Mililani St

Merchant St

Richards St

Queen St

Halekauwila St

38 ⊙

Alakea St

Reed La

14 ⊗

Bishop St

13 ⊗

Ala Moana Blvd

Aloha Tower Dr

92

Fort St

Pier 7

Pier 6

P

10 ⊙ Aloha
Tower

Pier 9

Pier 8

For reviews see	
⊙ Top Sights	p24
⊙ Sights	p30
⊗ Eating	p34
⊙⊙ Drinking	p38
⊙ Entertainment	p40
⊙ Shopping	p42

Sights

State Capitol
NOTABLE BUILDING

1 Map p28, E5

Built in the architecturally interesting 1960s, Hawaii's state capitol is a poster child of conceptual postmodernism: two cone-shaped legislative chambers have sloping walls to represent volcanoes; the supporting columns shaped like coconut palms symbolize the eight main islands; and a large encircling pool represents the Pacific Ocean surrounding Hawaii. Visitors are free to walk through the open-air rotunda and peer through viewing windows into the legislative chambers. Pick up a self-guided tour brochure on the 4th floor from Room 415. (☏808-586-0178; 415 S Beretania St; admission free; ⏲7:45am-4:30pm Mon-Fri)

Father Damien Statue
STATUE

2 Map p28, E5

In front of the capitol is a highly stylized statue of Father Damien, the Belgian priest who lived and worked with victims of Hansen's disease (leprosy) who were exiled to the island of Moloka'i during the late 19th century, before later dying of the disease himself. In 2009 the Catholic Church canonized Father Damien as Hawaii's first saint after the allegedly miraculous recovery from cancer in 1988 of a Honolulu schoolteacher who had prayed over Damien's original grave site on Moloka'i.

Hawai'i State Art Museum
MUSEUM

3 Map p28, D4

With its vibrant, thought-provoking collections, this public art museum brings together traditional and contemporary art from Hawaii's multiethnic communities. The museum inhabits a grand 1928 Spanish Mission Revival–style building, formerly a YMCA and today a nationally registered historic site. (☏808-586-0900; www.hawaii.gov/sfca; 2nd fl, No 1 Capitol District Bldg, 250 S Hotel St; admission free; ⏲10am-4pm Tue-Sat, also 6-9pm 1st Fri each month)

Ali'iolani Hale
HISTORIC BUILDING

4 Map p28, C6

The first major government building ordered by the Hawaiian monarchy in 1874, the 'House of Heavenly Kings' was designed by Australian architect Thomas Rowe to be a royal palace, although it was never used as such. Today, it houses the Supreme Court of Hawai'i. Go through the security checkpoint and step inside the King Kamehameha V Judiciary History Center, where you can browse thought-provoking historical displays about martial law during WWII and the reign of Kamehameha I. (☏808-539-4999; www.jhchawaii.net; 417 S King St; admission free; ⏲8am-4.30pm Mon-Fri)

SHANEFF CARL / GETTY IMAGES ©

Ali'iolani Hale and the Kamehameha the Great Statue

Kamehameha the Great Statue

STATUE

5  Map p28, D6

Standing before the Ali'iolani Hale, a bronze statue of Kamehameha the Great faces 'Iolani Palace. Often ceremonially draped with layers of flower lei, the statue was cast in 1880 in Florence, Italy, by American sculptor Thomas Gould. The current statue is a recast, as the first statue was lost at sea near the Falkland Islands. It was dedicated here in 1883, just a decade before the Hawaiian monarchy would be overthrown.

Kawaiaha'o Church

CHURCH

6  Map p28, D7

Nicknamed 'Westminster Abbey of the Pacific,' O'ahu's oldest church was built on the site where the first missionaries constructed a grass thatch church shortly after their arrival in 1820. The original structure seated 300 Hawaiians on *lauhala* mats, woven from hala (screwpine) leaves. This 1842 New England Gothic–style church is made of 14,000 coral slabs, which divers chiseled out of O'ahu's underwater reefs – a weighty task that took four years. (☑808-469-3000; www. kawaiahao.org; 957 Punchbowl St; admission free; ☺usually 8:30am-4pm Mon-Fri, worship service 9am Sun)

Hawaiian Mission Houses Historic Site and Archives

MUSEUM

7 ⦿ Map p28, E7

Occupying the original headquarters of the Sandwich Islands mission that forever changed the course of Hawaiian history, this modest museum is authentically furnished with handmade quilts on the beds and iron cooking pots in the stone fireplaces. You'll need to take a guided tour to peek inside any of the buildings. (📞808-447-3910; www.missionhouses.org; 553 S King St; 1hr guided tour adult/child 6-18yr & college student with ID $10/6; ⏱10am-4pm Tue-Sat, guided tours usually 11am, noon, 1pm, 2pm & 3pm)

Top Tip

Tantulus-Round Top Scenic Drive

Starting above downtown Honolulu and the H-1 Fwy, this 10-mile circuit is a loop called Tantalus Dr on its western side, Round Top Dr to the east.

Offering skyline views to drivers and cyclists alike, the twisting road climbs almost to the top of Mt Tantalus (2013ft), aka Pu'u 'Ohi'a. Bamboo, ginger, elephant-eared taro and eucalyptus trees make up the roadside profusion of tropical plants. Many hiking trails branch off the loop, which passes by Pu'u 'Ualaka'a State Wayside, with its magnificent views, on the descent.

Washington Place

HISTORIC BUILDING

8 ⦿ Map p28, E4

Formerly the governor's official residence, this colonial-style mansion was built in 1846 by US sea captain John Dominis. The captain's son became the governor of O'ahu and married the Hawaiian princess who later became Queen Lili'uokalani. After the queen was released from house arrest inside 'Iolani Palace in 1896, she lived here until her death in 1917. A plaque near the sidewalk is inscribed with the lyrics to 'Aloha 'Oe,' the patriotic anthem she composed. (📞808-586-0240; http://governor.hawaii.gov/about/historic-washington-place/; 320 S Beretania St; admission free; ⏱tours by appointment only, usually at 10am Thu)

Cathedral of St Andrew

CHURCH

9 ⦿ Map p28, E4

King Kamehameha IV, attracted to the royal Church of England, decided to build his own cathedral and founded the Anglican Church in Hawaii in 1861. The cathedral's cornerstone was laid in 1867, four years after his death on St Andrew's Day – hence the church's name. The architecture is French Gothic, utilizing stone and stained glass shipped from England. For a free lunchtime concert, the largest pipe organ in the Pacific is sonorously played every Friday at 12.15pm. (📞808-524-2822; www.saintandrewscathedral.net; 229 Queen Emma Sq; admission free; ⏱usually 8:30am-4pm Mon-Fri, tours 11:50am Sun; Ⓟ)

Aloha Tower
LANDMARK

10 Map p28, A5

Built in 1926, this 10-story landmark was once the city's tallest building. In the golden days when all tourists to Hawaii arrived by ship, this pre-WWII waterfront icon – with its four-sided clock tower inscribed with 'Aloha' – greeted every visitor. These days, Hawaii Pacific University has bought the Aloha Tower Marketplace and is revitalizing it for retail, dining and student housing. Take the elevator to the top-floor tower observation deck for 360-degree views of Honolulu and the waterfront. (www.alohatower.com; 1 Aloha Tower Dr; admission free; ⏱9:30am-5pm; 🅿)

Foster Botanical Garden
GARDENS

11 Map p28, D1

Tropical plants you've only ever read about can be spotted in all their glory at this botanic garden, which took root in 1850. Among its rarest specimens are the Hawaiian *loulu* palm and the East African *Gigasiphon macrosiphon*, both thought to be extinct in the wild. Several of the garden's towering trees are the largest of their kind in the USA. (☎808-522-7066; www.honolulu.gov/parks/hbg.html; 180 N Vineyard Blvd; adult/child 6-12yr $5/1; ⏱9am-4pm, guided tours usually 1pm Mon-Sat; 🅿)

National Memorial Cemetery of the Pacific
CEMETERY

12 Map p28, E3

Northeast of downtown Honolulu is a bowl-shaped crater, nicknamed the Punchbowl, formed by a long-extinct volcano. Hawaiians called the crater Puowaina ('hill of human sacrifices'). It's believed that at an ancient heiau here the slain bodies of *kapu* (taboo) breakers were ceremonially cremated upon an altar. Today the remains of ancient Hawaiians sacrificed to appease the gods share the crater floor with the bodies of nearly 50,000 soldiers, many of whom were killed in the Pacific during WWII. (☎808-532-3720; www.cem.va.gov/cems/nchp/nmcp.asp; 2177 Puowaina Dr; admission free; ⏱8am-5:30pm Sep 30-Mar 1, 8am-6:30pm Mar 2-Sep 29; 🅿)

Eating

Bishop St Cafe

JAPANESE, ITALIAN $

13 Map p28, B5

Offering up lunches to Downtown workers in an extremely convivial setting, Bishop St Cafe is one of those lovely fusion places, serving equally good Japanese and Italian cuisine. There's outside courtyard seating in the historic Dillingham Transportation Building. Choices range from Japanese *udon* or *soba* noodles to paninis and pastas. (☎808-537-6951; www.facebook.com/bishopstreetcafe; 725 Bishop St; mains $7-15; ☺11am-3pm Mon-Fri)

Hiroshi Eurasian Tapas

FUSION $$

14 Map p28, C8

A serious player on the Honolulu culinary scene, chef Hiroshi Fukui puts a Japanese twist on Pacific Rim fusion style, from crab cannelloni swirled with miso sauce to smoked *hamachi* (yellow-tail) with a garlicky habanero pepper kick. Order foamy tropical martinis and fresh-fruit sodas at the bar. Make reservations for dinner. (☎808-533-4476; www.hiroshihawaii.com; Waterfront Plaza, 500 Ala Moana Blvd; shared plates $9-17, mains $26-29; ☺5:30-9:30pm; P)

Hukilau

HAWAIIAN $$

15 Map p28, C4

Underground at downtown's only high-rise hotel, this sports bar and grill serves an aloha-shirt-wearing business crowd. Huge salads, sandwiches and burgers aren't as tempting as only-in-Hawaii specialties such as miso butterfish, *kimchi* (Korean seasoned vegetable pickle dish) and *kalua* (cooked in an underground pit) pig *saimin* (noodle soup) and ahi *poke*. Live music on most Friday nights. (☎808-523-3460; www.dahukilau.com/honolulu; Executive Centre, 1088 Bishop St; mains $11-20; ☺11am-2pm & 3-9pm Mon-Fri)

Vita Juice

HEALTH FOOD $

16 Map p28, C4

Flooded with Hawai'i Pacific University students, this orange-walled juice and smoothie bar takes the concept of 'brain food' seriously. Healthy ingredients range from Amazonian acai and Tibetan goji berries to green tea and

---

Hawaiian speciality *loco moco* (rice, fried egg and hamburger patty topped with gravy)

ginseng. (☎808-526-1396; www.freewebs.
com/vitajuice; 1111-C Fort St Mall; items $3-7;
⏰7am-5pm Mon-Fri; 🖊)

'Umeke Market
& Deli

SUPERMARKET $

17 🍴 Map p28, C4

Fresh, organic island produce, natural-
foods groceries and a vegetarian- and
vegan-friendly takeout deli counter for
healthy pick-me-ups such as kale and
quinoa salads, hummus sandwiches,
hoisin turkey meatloaf and iced *kom-
bucha* (effervescent tea). (☎808-522-
7377; www.umekemarket.com; 1001 Bishop
St; mains $4-10; ⏰7am-4pm Mon-Fri; 🖊)

Pho To-Chau

VIETNAMESE $

18 🍴 Map p28, B2

Always packed, this Vietnamese restaurant holds fast to its hard-earned
reputation for serving Honolulu's best
pho (Vietnamese noodle soup). With
beef, broth and vegetables the dish
is a complete meal in itself. It's so
popular that you may have to queue
underneath the battered-looking sign
outside to score one of a dozen or so
rickety wooden tables. (☎808-533-4549;
1007 River St; mains $7-10; ⏰8:30am-
2:30pm)

Mei Sum

CHINESE $

19 ✕ Map p28, C3

Where else can you go to satisfy that crazy craving for dim sum in the afternoon or evening (which maybe aren't as fresh as they are in the morning)? For over a decade, this no-nonsense corner stop has been cranking out a multitude of cheap little plates and a full spread of Chinese mains. (📞 808-531-3268; 1170 Nu'uanu Ave; dim-sum dishes $2-4, mains $8-23; ⏱8am-9pm Mon-Fri, from 7am Sat & Sun)

Mabuhay Cafe & Restaurant

FILIPINO $

20 ✕ Map p28, B2

The tablecloths, well-worn counter stools and jukebox should clue you in that this is a mom-and-pop joint. They've been cooking pots of succulent, garlic-laden pork *adobo* (meat marinated in vinegar and garlic) and *kare-kare* (oxtail stew) on this corner by the river since the 1960s. (📞 808-545-1956; 1049 River St; mains $6-13; ⏱10am-9pm Mon-Sat)

Downbeat Diner & Lounge

DINER $

21 ✕ Map p28, B3

Shiny late-night diner with lipstick-red booths posts a vegetarian- and vegan-friendly menu of salads, sandwiches, grilled burgers and heaping island-style breakfasts such as *loco moco* (rice, fried egg and hamburger patty) and Portuguese sweet-bread French toast. The lounge, running a full bar, features live music three to four times per week. (📞 808-533-2328; www.downbeatdiner.com; 42 N Hotel St; mains $5-15; ⏱11am-midnight Mon, to 3am Tue-Thu, to 4am Fri & Sat, to 10pm Sun; 🍷🎵)

Little Village Noodle House

CHINESE $$

22 ✕ Map p28, B3

Forget about chop suey. If you live for anything fishy in black-bean sauce, this is Honolulu's gold standard. On the eclectic pan-Chinese menu, regional dishes are served up garlicky,

---

Understand
Hawaii's State Flag

You may notice that Hawaii's state flag is quartered, with the Union Jack in the top left corner next to the flagpole. (You can see one in downtown Honolulu's historic capitol district.) But Hawaii was never part of the British Commonwealth. Kamehameha the Great simply thought the Union Jack would add an element of regal splendor to Hawaii's flag, so he took the liberty of adding it. The flag's eight horizontal red, white and blue stripes represent the eight main islands. Today Native Hawaiian sovereignty activists often choose to fly the state flag upside down, a time-honored symbol of distress.

fiery or with just the right dose of salt-iness. For a cross-cultural combo, fork into sizzling butterfish or roasted pork with island-grown taro. Reservations recommended. (808-545-3008; 1113 Smith St; mains $8-22; 10:30am-10:30pm Sun-Thu, to midnight Fri & Sat; ❄)

Soul de Cuba
CUBAN $$

23 Map p28, C3

Nowhere else in Honolulu can you sate your craving for Afro-Cuban food and out-of-this-world *mojitos* except at this hip resto-lounge near Chinatown's art galleries. Stick with family-recipe classics such as *ropa vieja* (shredded beef in tomato sauce), *bocadillos* (sandwiches, served until 5pm) and black-bean soup. Reservations recommended. (808-545-2822; www.souldecuba.com; 1121 Bethel St; mains $10-24; 11am-10pm Mon-Thu, to 11pm Fri & Sat, to 9pm Sun)

The Pig & the Lady
ASIAN, FUSION $$

24 Map p28, B3

An award-winning Vietnamese Fusion restaurant where you'll need to book for an evening meal, The Pig & the Lady is one of the hottest new places to dine on the island. Imaginative lunch sandwiches come with shrimp chips or *pho* broth, while delicious dinner options include Laotian fried chicken and dipping-style *pho tsuku-men*. (808-585-8255; http://thepigand thelady.com; 83 N King St; mains $10-25;

 Top Tip

Hawaii Food Tours

The guys at **Hawaii Food Tours** (808-926-3663; www.hawaiifood-tours.com; tours from $119) offer two extremely popular tours. The five-hour 'Hole-in-the-Wall' tour hits all sorts of spots around Honolulu such as Chinatown, island plate-lunch stops, beloved baker-ies, crack-seed candy shops and more. The seven- to eight-hour 'North Shore Food Tour' heads to the other side of the island. Tours include food, fun and transporta-tion. Reservations are essential.

10.30am-2pm Mon-Sat plus 5.30-9.30pm Tue-Thu, to midnight Fri & Sat)

Lucky Belly
ASIAN, FUSION $$

25 Map p28, B3

Where Japanese pop art hangs over sleek bistro tables packed elbows-to-shoulders, this arts-district noodle bar crafts hot and spicy Asian fusion bites, knock-out artisanal cocktails and amazingly fresh, almost architectural salads that the whole table can share. A 'Belly Bowl' of ramen soup topped with buttery pork belly, smoked bacon and pork sausage is carnivore heaven. (808-531-1888; www.luckybelly.com; 50 N Hotel St; mains $8-14; 11am-2pm & 5pm-midnight Mon-Sat)

Local Life

Cafe Julia

In the charming old YWCA Laniakea building opposite ʻIolani Palace, **Cafe Julia** (Map p28, C5; ☏808-533-3334; http://cafejuliahawaii.com; 1040 Richards St; mains $10-28; ⊗11am-2pm Mon-Fri. plus 4-9pm Wed-Fri, 9am-1pm & 4-9pm Sun) is a gem. Named after Julia Morgan, one of the America's first female architects, who designed the building, the service and cuisine is superb. In an open-air setting, it's perfect for *poke* tacos or garlic *ahi* for lunch, or settling into a few cocktails in the evening.

Duc's Bistro   FUSION $$

26 Map p28, C2

Honolulu's bigwigs hang out after work at this swank French-Vietnamese bistro with a tiny bar. Ignore the surrounding seedy streets and step inside this culinary oasis for buttery escargot, *bánh xèo* (Vietnamese crepes), pan-fried fish with green mango relish, and fire-roasted eggplant. A small jazz combo serenades diners some evenings. Reservations recommended. (☏808-531-6325; www.ducsbistro.com; 1188 Maunakea St; mains $16-26; ⊗11am-2pm Mon-Fri, 5-10pm daily)

Drinking

Manifest   BAR, CAFE

27 Map p28, C3

Smack in the middle of Chinatown's art scene, this lofty apartment-like space adorned with provocative photos and paintings doubles as a serene coffee shop by day and a cocktail bar by night, hosting movie and trivia nights and DJ sets (no cover). Foamy cappuccinos and spicy chais are daytime perfection. (http://manifesthawaii.com; 32 N Hotel St; ⊗8am-2am Mon-Fri, 10am-2am Sat; 🛜)

Beach Bum Cafe   CAFE

28 Map p28, C4

Right in downtown's high-rise financial district, this connoisseur's coffee bar serves 100% organic, grown-in-Hawaii beans, roasted in small batches and hand-brewed just one ideal cup at a time. Chat up the baristas while you sip the rich flavors of the Big Island, Maui, Kauaʻi and even Molokaʻi. Also has an outpost at the First Hawaiian Center down the road. (☏808-521-6699; www.beachbumcafe.com; 1088 Bishop St; ⊗6:30am-5pm Mon-Fri; 🛜)

Honolulu Coffee Company   COFFEE SHOP

29 Map p28, C5

Overlooking Tamarind Sq with city skyline views, here you can take a break from tramping around

LINDA CHING / GETTY IMAGES ©

Tropical drinks from a Honolulu bar

Honolulu's historical sites for a java jolt brewed from handpicked, hand-roasted 100% Kona estate-grown beans. Also at Ala Moana Center and in Waikiki. (☏808-521-4400; www.honolulucoffee.com; 1001 Bishop St; ⏱6am-5:30pm Mon-Fri, 7am-noon Sat; 🛜)

Tea at 1024 TEAHOUSE

30 Map p28, B3

Tea at 1024 takes you back in time to another era. Cutesy sandwiches, scones and cakes accompany your choice of tea as you relax and watch the Chinatown crowd rush by the window. They even have bonnets for you to don to add to the ambience. Set menus run from $20.95 per person and reservations are recommended. (☏808-521-9596; www.teaat1024.net; 1024 Nu'uanu Ave; ⏱11am-2pm Tue-Fri, to 3pm Sat)

Hank's Cafe BAR

31 Map p28, B3

You can't get more low-key than this neighborhood dive bar on the edge of Chinatown. Owner Hank is a jack-of-all-trades when it comes to the barfly business: the walls are decorated with Polynesian-themed art, live music rolls in some nights and regulars practically call it home. (☏808-526-1410; http://hankscafehawaii.com; 1038 Nu'uanu Ave; ⏱7am-2am)

Bar 35

BAR

32 Map p28, B3

Filled with aloha, this indoor-outdoor watering hole has a dizzying 100 domestic and international bottled beers to choose from, plus addictive chef-made gourmet fusion pizzas to go with all the brews. There's live music or DJs some weekend nights. (808-537-3535; http://bar35hawaii.com; 35 N Hotel St; 4pm-2am Mon-Fri, 6pm-2am Sat)

Fix Sports Lounge & Nightclub

NIGHTCLUB

33 Map p28, C3

These guys have got the bases covered with a cavernous sports lounge full of large flatscreens offering the standard sports-lounge fare...morphing into a raging nightclub later on with DJs and dancing. One of the largest venues on O'ahu. (808-728-4416; http://thefixsports loungeandnightclub.com; 80 S Pau'ahi St; 11am-2am Mon-Fri, 5pm-2am Sat)

Next Door

NIGHTCLUB, LOUNGE

34 Map p28, B3

Situated on a skid-row block of N Hotel St where dive bars are still the order of the day, this svelte cocktail lounge is a brick-walled retreat with vivid red couches and flickering candles. DJs spin house, hip hop, funk, mash-ups and retro sounds, while on other nights loud, live local bands play just about anything. (808-852-2243; www.facebook.com/nextdoorhi; 43 N Hotel St; 7pm-2am Wed-Sat)

Entertainment

Dragon Upstairs

LIVE MUSIC

Right above Hank's Cafe (see 31 Map p28, B3) in Chinatown, this claustrophobic hideaway with a sedate older vibe and lots of funky artwork and mirrors hosts a rotating lineup of jazz cats, blues strummers and folk singers, usually on Thursday, Friday and Saturday nights. Occasional $5 cover charge. (808-526-1411; http://thedragonupstairs. com; 2nd fl, 1038 Nu'uanu Ave; usually 7pm-2am)

ARTS at Marks Garage

PERFORMING ARTS

35 Map p28, C3

On the cutting edge of the Chinatown arts scene, this community gallery and performance space puts on a variety of live shows, from stand-up comedy, burlesque cabaret nights and conversations with island artists to live jazz

Understand
History of Honolulu

First Discoveries

The first wave of Polynesians, most likely from the Marquesas Islands, voyaged by canoe to the Hawaiian Islands 300–600AD. A second wave, this time from Tahiti, arrived 1000–1300AD. Captain Cook, the first foreigner known to reach the islands, visited Hawaii twice in 1778–79 and was killed on the Big Island. O'ahu's fall to Kamehameha the Great in 1795 signaled the beginning of a united Hawaiian kingdom. Kamehameha moved his royal court to Honolulu ('Sheltered Bay').

Foreigners & Sugar

In 1793, the English frigate *Butterworth* became the first foreign ship to sail into what is now Honolulu Harbor. In the 1820s, Honolulu's first bars and brothels opened to international whaling crews just as prudish Protestant missionaries began arriving from New England. Honolulu replaced Lahaina as the capital of the kingdom of Hawai'i in 1845.

In the 1830s, sugar became king of O'ahu's industry. Plantation workers from Asia and Europe were brought to fill the island's labor shortage. The 19th century ended with the Hawaiian monarchy violently overthrown at Honolulu's 'Iolani Palace, creating a short-lived independent republic dominated by sugar barons and ultimately annexed by the USA.

War in the Pacific

After the bombing of Pearl Harbor on December 7, 1941, O'ahu was placed under martial law during WWII. As many civil rights were suspended, a detention center for Japanese Americans and resident aliens was established on Honolulu's Sand Island. The US federal government didn't apologize for these injustices until 1988.

Post-WWII

After WWII, jet-age travel and baby-boom prosperity provided O'ahu with a thriving tourism business to replace its declining shipping industry. In the 1970s, the Hawaiian renaissance flowered, especially on the University of Hawai'i at Manoa campus and after the successful wayfaring voyage of the *Hokule'a* canoe to Tahiti.

By the 1980s, rampant tourist development had overbuilt Waikiki and turned some of O'ahu's agricultural land into water-thirsty golf courses and sprawling resorts. The island's last sugar mills closed in the 1990s, leaving O'ahu more heavily dependent on tourism than ever.

Local Life

Tin Can Mailman

Fans of vintage tiki wares and 20th-century Hawaiiana books will fall in love with **Tin Can Mailman** (Map p28, B3; http://tincanmailman.net; 1026 Nu'uanu Ave; ☉11am-5pm Mon-Thu, to 9pm Fri, to 4pm Sat), a little Chinatown antiques shop. Treasures include jewelry and ukuleles, silk aloha shirts, tropical-wood furnishings, vinyl records, rare prints and tourist brochures from the post-WWII tourism boom. No photos allowed, sorry.

and Hawaiian music. (☎808-521-2903; www.artsatmarks.com; 1159 Nu'uanu Ave; ☉11am-6pm Tue-Sat)

Kumu Kahua Theatre
PERFORMING ARTS

36 ⭐ Map p28, B4

In the restored Kamehameha V Post Office building, this little 100-seat treasure is dedicated to premiering works by Hawaii's playwrights, with themes focusing on contemporary multicultural island life, often richly peppered with Hawaiian pidgin. (☎808-536-4441; www.kumukahua.org; 46 Merchant St)

Shopping

Cindy's Lei Shoppe
ARTS, CRAFTS

37 Map p28, B3

At this inviting little shop, a Chinatown landmark, you can watch aunties craft flower lei made of orchids, plumeria, twining maile, lantern *'ilima* (flowering ground-cover) and ginger. Several other lei shops clustered nearby will also pack lei for you to carry back home on the plane. (☎808-536-6538; www.cindysleishoppe. com; 1034 Maunakea St; ☉usually 6am-6pm Mon-Sat, to 5pm Sun)

Kamaka Hawaii
MUSIC

38 Map p28, C8

Skip right by those tacky souvenir shops selling cheap plastic and wooden ukuleles. Kamaka specializes in handcrafted ukuleles made on O'ahu since 1916, with prices starting at around $500. Its signature is an oval-shaped 'pineapple' ukulele, which has a more mellow sound. Call ahead for free 30-minute factory tours, usually starting at 10:30am Tuesday through Friday. (☎808-531-3165; www. kamakahawaii.com; 550 South St; ☉8am-4pm Mon-Fri)

Artisan weaving *haku* lei at Cindy's Lei Shoppe

Madre Chocolate · FOOD

39 🔒 Map p28, C3

The Honolulu outpost of this Kailua chocolate company is serving up a storm in Chinatown with free samplings of such innovative flavors as Lili'koi Passionfruit and Coconut Milk & Caramelized Ginger Chocolate. A must for chocolate-lovers but it don't come cheap! If you're really keen, it even offers a five-day 'Experience Hawaiian Cacao & Chocolate Bootcamp' on O'ahu. (📞808-377-6440; http://madrechocolate.com; 8 N Pau'ahi St; ⏱11am-8pm Tue-Sat, to 6pm Mon)

Explore

Ala Moana & Around

Ala Moana means 'Path to the Sea' and its namesake road, Ala Moana Blvd, connects the coast between Waikiki and Honolulu. Although most people think of Ala Moana only for its shopping mall, Ala Moana Regional Park – O'ahu's biggest beach park – makes a relaxing alternative to crowded Waikiki, and a bevy of locally famous restaurants hide out in the area.

The Sights in a Day

☀ Start out with a coffee at **Fresh Cafe** (p48), but make sure to give yourself plenty of time at the enthralling **Honolulu Museum of Art** (p46). Take a break when needed at the excellent **Honolulu Museum of Art Cafe** (p54).

☀ Your afternoon will include some shopping and sun. Browse the shops at **Ward Warehouse** (p56) and Ward Center – don't miss **Native Books/Nā Mea Hawaii** (p49). Wander across to **Ala Moana Beach Park** (p49) for some time on the beach. It won't be long before the **Ala Moana Center** (p49) beckons.

☾ Grab dinner and drinks up at **Mai Tai Bar** (p49) on the Ho'okipa Tce of the shopping center. Your day wouldn't be complete without a sunset stroll around **Magic Island** back out at the beach park.

For a local's day in Ala Moana, see p48.

 Top Sights

Honolulu Museum of Art (p46)

 Local Life

Culture & Sun at Ala Moana (p48)

💜 **Best of Honolulu**

Beaches
Ala Moana Beach Park (p49)

Eating
Kaka'ako Kitchen (p49)

Alan Wong's (p53)

Drinking & Entertainment
Republik (p56)

Jazz Minds Art & Café (p56)

Museums
Honolulu Museum of Art (p46)

Hawaiiana Shopping
Native Books/Nā Mea Hawaii (p49)

Manuheali'i (p57)

Getting There

🚌 **Bus** The Ala Moana Mall is O'ahu's central transfer point for TheBus. Buses head out in all directions from here.

🚗 **Car** Ala Moana Blvd runs from Downtown through Ala Moana to Waikiki. There is free parking at the Ala Moana Center, Ward Warehouse and Ward Center. Also at Ala Moana Beach Park.

Top Sights
Honolulu Museum of Art

This exceptional fine-arts museum may be the biggest surprise of your trip to Oʻahu. Dating to 1927, it has a classical facade that's invitingly open and airy, with galleries branching off a series of garden and water-fountain courtyards. Stunningly beautiful exhibits reflect the various cultures that make up contemporary Hawaii, include one of the country's finest Asian art collections. The Arts of Hawaii exhibition is especially captivating. You'll also find originals by van Gogh, Gauguin, Cezanne, Monet, Matisse and Whistler.

Map p50, C1

📞 808-532-8700

www.honolulumuseum.org

900 S Beretania St

adult/child $10/free, free 1st Wed & 3rd Sun each month

🕙 10am-4:30pm Tue-Sat, 1-5pm Sun 🅿 ♿

Honolulu Museum of Art at Spalding House, featuring artwork by Deborah Butterfield

Don't Miss

Museum Events

Check the museum website for upcoming special events, including: gallery tours and art lectures; film screenings and music concerts at the Doris Duke Theatre; ARTafterDARK (www.artafterdark. org) parties with food, drinks and live entertainment on the last Friday of some months; and family-friendly arts and cultural programs on the third Sunday of every month.

The Museum Shop

As you would expect, the Museum shop offers fine works by Hawaii artisans and designers that you won't find outside of the islands. This is the place to find that unique souvenir of quality that you may have been looking for. Also available are publications, prints, posters and stationery that reflect the international scope of the museum's collections.

Honolulu Museum of Art at Spalding House

Admission tickets are also valid for same-day visits to the Honolulu Museum of Art at **Spalding House** (☎808-526-1322; www.honoluluacademy.org; 2411 Makiki Heights Dr; adult/child 4-17yr $10/free, 1st Wed of the month free; ⏰10am-4pm Tue-Sat, noon-4pm Sun; P), a sprawling estate mansion high in Makiki Heights that features stunning views, sculpture and flower gardens, and its most prized piece, an environmental installation by David Hockney based on his sets for Ravel's opera *L'Enfant et les sortilèges*.

Honolulu Museum of Art at First Hawaiian Center

First Hawaiian Bank's **high-rise headquarters** (☎808-526-0232; www.honoluluacademy.org; admission free; ⏰8:30am-4:30pm Mon-Thu, to 6pm Fri) in Downtown also houses a gallery of the Honolulu Museum of Art. It features fascinating mixed-media exhibits of modern and contemporary works by artists from around Hawaii. Even the building itself features a four-story-high glass wall incorporating 185 prisms.

☑ Top Tips

▶ In partnership with the Doris Duke Foundation for Islamic Art, the museum serves as the orientation center for tours of Shangri La (p98). Two and a half hour tours, beginning and ending at the Museum, can be booked online. Shangri La has no public access and the only way to see it is on a tour organized through the Honolulu Museum of Art.

▶ Parking at the Honolulu Museum of Art School, diagonally opposite the museum at 1111 Victoria St (enter off Beretania or Young Sts), costs $5 for up to 5 hours.

✕ Take a Break

In a delightful open-air courtyard setting, the Honolulu Museum of Art Cafe (p54) focuses on serving market-fresh salads using O'ahu-grown ingredients from Tuesday to Saturday.

Local Life
Culture & Sun in Ala Moana

There's a lot more to the Ala Moana area than just the Ala Moana Center and the locals certainly know it. The Ward Center and Ward Warehouse offer excellent eating and browsing options, while Ala Moana Beach Park and Magic Island are stunners that many staying in Waikiki don't even realize are there!

1 Fresh Cafe

Start your morning at **Fresh Cafe** (☎808-688-8055; http://freshcafehi. com; 831 Queen St; ⊙8am-11pm Mon-Sat, 9am-6pm Sun; ☜), an alternative coffeehouse in an industrial warehouse area. No, you're not lost. Artists, bohemians and hipster hangers-on sip Vietnamese coffee, *pikake* iced tea, and Thai or *haupia*-flavored lattes here. When you're ready to walk, wander out to Ward Ave.

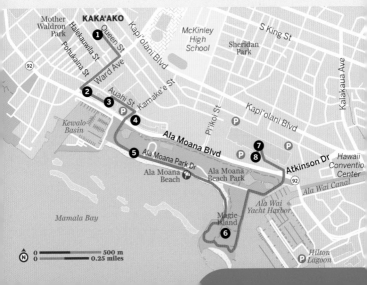

2 Native Books/Nā Mea Hawaii

In the Ward Warehouse complex, head in to **Native Books/Nā Mea Hawaii** (☎808-597-8967; www.nativebookshawaii.com; Ward Warehouse, 1050 Ala Moana Blvd; ⏱10am-8:30pm Mon-Thu, to 9pm Fri & Sat, to 6pm Sun). This place is a cultural gathering spot. Check online for special events before you go, including author readings, live local music and cultural classes.

3 Nohea Gallery

Head further east in the complex to find **Nohea Gallery** (www.noheagallery.com; Ward Warehouse, 1050 Ala Moana Blvd; ⏱10am-9pm Mon-Sat, to 6pm Sun). This high-end gallery sells handcrafted jewelry, glassware, pottery and woodwork, all of it made in Hawaii. Local artisans occasionally give demonstrations of their crafts on the sidewalk outside.

4 Kaka'ako Kitchen

Carry on along Auahi St to the Ward Center complex to find **Kaka'ako Kitchen** (☎808-596-7488; http://kakaakokitchen.com; Ward Center, 1200 Ala Moana Blvd; meals $7-15; ⏱10am-9pm Mon-Thu, to 10pm Fri & Sat, to 5pm Sun; Ⓟ♿). As *'ono* (delicious) as always, this popular counter joint dishes up healthy minded plate lunches with brown rice and organic greens. For a local deli twist, get the tempura mahimahi (white-fleshed fish) sandwich on a homemade taro bun.

5 Ala Moana Beach Park

It's time for some sun. Head out to **Ala Moana Beach Park** (1201 Ala Moana Blvd; Ⓟ♿), which boasts a broad, golden-sand beach – hugely popular, yet big enough that it never feels too crowded. This is where Honolulu residents come to run after work, play beach volleyball and enjoy weekend picnics. The park has full facilities, including lighted tennis courts.

6 Magic Island

The peninsula jutting from the southeast side of Ala Moana Beach Park park is **Magic Island**. Year-round, you can take an idyllic sunset walk around the peninsula's perimeter, within an anchor's toss of sailboats pulling in and out of neighboring Ala Wai Yacht Harbor. A great spot from which to watch the fireworks on Friday nights.

7 Ala Moana Shopping Center

Head over and into the **Ala Moana Shopping Center** (www.alamoanacenter.com; 1450 Ala Moana Blvd; ⏱9.30am-9pm Mon-Sat, 10am-7pm Sun) for some respite from the sun. This open-air shopping mall and its nearly 300 department stores and mostly chain stores could compete on an international runway with some of Asia's famous mega-malls. Plenty to look at and a great spot for people-watching.

8 Mai Tai Bar

It must be time for a cold drink! Head upstairs in the Ala Moana Shopping-Center to **Mai Tai Bar** (☎808-947-2900; www.maitaibar.com; Ho'okipa Tce, 3rd fl, Ala Moana Center, 1450 Ala Moana Blvd; ⏱11am-1am; 🛜). During sunset and late-night happy hours, this enormous tropical bar is packed with a see-and-flirt crowd. Island-style live music plays nightly.

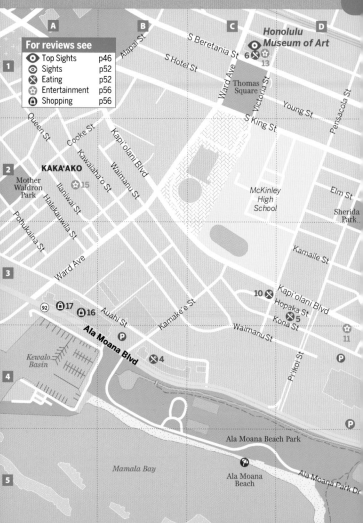

Honolulu Museum of Art

For reviews see
◉ Top Sights	p46
◉ Sights	p52
✖ Eating	p52
☆ Entertainment	p56
🔒 Shopping	p56

A B C D

Alapai St
S Beretania St
S Hotel St
Ward Ave
Thomas Square
S King St
Victoria St
Young St
Pensacola St

6
13

Queen St
Cooke St
Kapi'olani Blvd
Kawaiaha'o St
Waimanu St

KAKA'AKO
15

Mother Waldron Park
Ilaniwai St
Halekauwila St

McKinley High School
Elm St
Sheridan Park

Pohukaina St
Ward Ave

Kamaile St

Kapi'olani Blvd
10
Hopaka St
Kona St
5

92
17
16
Auahi St
Kamake'e St
Waimanu St
Pi'ikoi St
11

Ala Moana Blvd
4

Kewalo Basin

Ala Moana Beach Park

Mamala Bay
Ala Moana Beach
Ala Moana Park Dr

E
F
G
H

H1

Lunalilo St
Lunalilo Fwy
Matlock Ave
Kinau St
S Beretania St
Prikoi St
Alder St
Birch St
S King St
Rycroft St
Sheridan St
Liona St
Ahana St
Rycroft St
Kanunu St
Keʻeaumoku St
Makaloa St
Kaheka St
Kona St
Mahukona St
Atkinson Dr
Ala Moana Blvd
Ala Wai Yacht Harbor

Keʻeaumoku St
Makiki St
Makiki District Park
Cartwright Park
Kalakaua Ave

Punahou St
S Beretania St
Young St
S King St
Waiola St
Citron St
Hauoli St
Pumehana St
Lime St
Water Giver Statue
Hawaii Convention Center
Ala Wai Canal
Kalakaua Ave

Punahou School
Wilder Ave
Dole St
H1
Artesian St
Algaroba St
McCully St
Date St
Fern St
Willwill St
Kapiʻolani Blvd
Ala Wai Blvd
Ala Wai Park

500 m
0.25 miles

7
18
9
3
14
8
2
12
1

92

Sights

Water Giver Statue
STATUE

1 Map p50, G5

Fronting the Honolulu Convention Center, this magnificent statue symbolically acknowledges the Hawaiian people for their generosity and expressions of goodwill to newcomers. Its sister-statue is the Storyteller Statue in Waikiki. (1801 Kalakaua Ave, Hawaii Convention Center)

Eating

Yataimura
JAPANESE $

2 Map p50, E4

Head to the upper level of the Ala Moana Center's Japanese department store Shirokiya to unlock a beer garden and boisterous food-stall marketplace that's a gold mine of takeout meals, from *bentō* boxes to hot *takoyaki* (fried minced-octopus balls). (www.shirokiya. com; 2nd fl, Shirokiya, Ala Moana Center, 1450 Ala Moana Blvd; items $2-12; ⊙10am-10pm)

Makai Market
FAST FOOD $

3 Map p50, E4

Let your preconceptions about mall food courts fly out the window at these Asian-fusion-flavored indoor food stalls. Dig into Yummy Korean BBQ, Donburi Don-Don for Japanese rice bowls or the island-flavored Lahaina Chicken Company and Ala Moana Poi Bowl. (1st fl, Ala Moana Center, 1450 Ala Moana Blvd; mains $6-12; ⊙8am-8pm; ♿)

Kua 'Aina
FAST FOOD $

4 Map p50, B4

Shopping-mall outpost of Hale'iwa's gourmet burger joint serves crispy matchstick fries, pineapple and avocado beef burgers, and grilled ahi and veggie sandwiches for hungry crowds. Also in Kapolei. (☎808-591-9133; www.kua-aina.com; Ward Center,

---

Understand
Mr Obama's Neighborhood

During the 2008 race to elect the 44th president of the United States, Republican vice-presidential candidate Sarah Palin kept asking the country, 'Who is Barack Obama?' It was Obama's wife, Michelle, who had an answer ready: 'You can't really understand Barack until you understand Hawaii.'

Obama, who grew up in Honolulu's Makiki Heights neighborhood, inland and above the Ala Moana area, has written that 'Hawaii's spirit of tolerance... became an integral part of my world view, and a basis for the values I hold most dear.' The local media and many *kama'aina* (those who were born and grew up in Hawaii) agree that Hawaii's multiethnic social fabric helped shape the leader who created a rainbow coalition during the 2008 election.

ANN CECIL / GETTY IMAGES ©

Japanese plate lunch, Honolulu

1200 Ala Moana Blvd; burgers & sandwiches $5-10; ⊘10:30am-9pm Mon-Sat, to 8pm Sun; P♿)

Side Street Inn   HAWAIIAN $$

5 🍴 Map p50, D3

This late-night mecca is where you'll find Honolulu's top chefs hanging out after their own kitchens close, along with partyin' locals who come for hearty portions of *kalbi* and pan-fried pork chops. Make reservations and bring friends, or join the construction-worker crews ordering plate lunches at the takeout counter. Warning: big portions! (☎808-591-0253; http://side streetinn.com; 1225 Hopaka St; mains $7-20; ⊘2pm-midnight Sun-Thu, to 1am Fri & Sat)

☑ Top Tip

Eat at Alan Wong's

One of O'ahu's big-gun chefs, Alan Wong offers his creative interpretations of Hawaii Regional Cuisine with emphasis on fresh seafood and local produce at his eponymous **restaurant** (☎808-949-2526; www.alanwongs.com; 1857 S King St; mains $35-60; ⊘5-10pm). Order the time-tested signature dishes such as ginger-crusted *onaga* (red snapper), Kona lobster seafood stew and twice-cooked *kalbi* (short ribs). Make reservations for in-demand tables weeks in advance.

Honolulu Museum of Art Cafe

MODERN AMERICAN **$$**

6 Map p50, C1

Market-fresh salads and sandwiches made with Oʻahu-grown ingredients, a decent selection of wines by the glass and tropically infused desserts make this an indulgent way to support the arts. Romantic tables facing the sculpture courtyard fountain and underneath a monkeypod tree are equally well suited to dates or power-broker lunches. Reservations recommended. (☏808-532-8734; www.honoluluacademy. org; Honolulu Museum of Art, 900 S Beretania St; mains $11-22; ☺11:30am-1:30pm Tue-Sat)

Sorabol

KOREAN **$$**

7 Map p50, E3

Sorabol feeds lunching Korean ladies by day and bleary-eyed clubbers before dawn. Detractors often sniff that its reputation is undeserved, but the rest of the city has undying gratitude for this around-the-clock joint, often visited after midnight in a drunken

Local Life
Honolulu Farmers Market

At the **Honolulu Farmers Market** (Map p50, C2; http://hfbf.org/markets; Neal S Blaisdell Center, 777 Ward Ave; ☺4-7pm Wed; ☏☂) pick up anything from aquacultural seafood and Oʻahu honey to fresh fruit and tropical flowers, all trucked into the city by Hawaii Farm Bureau Federation members. Graze food stalls set up by island chefs, food artisans and Kona coffee roasters, too.

stupor. Marinated *kalbi* and steamed butterfish are specialties. Watch out for a late-night service charge (20%). (☏808-947-3113; www.sorabolhawaii.com; 805 Keʻeaumoku St; set meals $11-38; ☺24hr)

Shokudo

JAPANESE **$$**

8 Map p50, F4

Knock back lychee sake-tinis at this sleek, modern Japanese restaurant (*shokudō* means 'dining room') that's always filled to the rafters. A mixed-plate traditional Japanese and island-fusion menu depicts dozens of dishes, from *mochi* (rice cake) cheese gratin to lobster dynamite rolls, more traditional noodles and sushi, and silky house-made tofu. Reservations recommended. (☏808-941-3701; www.shokudojapanese. com; 1585 Kapiʻolani Blvd; shared plates $5-25; ☺11:30am-midnight Sun-Thu, to 1am Fri & Sat)

Chef Mavro

FUSION **$$$**

9 Map p50, H3

At Honolulu's most avant-garde restaurant, maverick chef George Mavrothalassitis creates conceptual dishes, all paired with Old and New World wines. Unfortunately the cutting-edge experimental cuisine, like the half-empty atmosphere, sometimes falls flat, although some will swear they've had the meal of a lifetime. Reservations essential. (☏808-944-4714; www. chefmavro.com; 1969 S King St; multicourse tasting menus from $95; ☺6-9pm Wed-Sun)

Nanzan Girogiro

JAPANESE **$$$**

10 Map p50, C3

Traditional *kaiseki ryōri* (seasonal small-course) cuisine infused with

Understand
Hawaii Cuisine

The Island 'Diet'

Before human contact, the only indigenous edibles in Hawaii were ferns and 'ohelo berries. The first Polynesians brought with them kalo (taro), 'ulu (breadfruit), 'uala (sweet potato), mai'a (banana), ko (sugarcane) and niu (coconut), plus chickens, pigs and dogs for meat – and they enjoyed an abundance of seafood. Western explorers dropped off cattle and horses, and later missionaries and settlers planted exotic fruits such as pineapple and guava. When the sugar industry peaked in the late 19th century, bringing waves of immigrant laborers from Asia and Europe, Hawaii's cuisine developed a taste and identity all its own. It took plantation imports, including rice, shōyu (soy sauce), ginger and chili pepper, but never abandoned Native Hawaiian staples like kalua pork and poi (pounded taro root). Today, Hawaii's food traditions are multiethnic. This tasty culinary mishmash has turned locals into adventurous and passionate eaters who are always hungry for that next knockout mouthful of 'ono kine grinds (good food).

Local Food

Cheap, filling and tasty, a local 'mixed plate lunch' includes two-scoop rice (almost always sticky white rice), a scoop of mayonnaise-laden macaroni salad and a hot, hearty main dish, such as Korean-style kalbi short ribs, Filipino pork adobo, batter-fried mochiko (Japanese rice-flour) chicken or furikake-encrusted mahimahi. Another local favorite is poke, which is bite-sized cubes of raw fish typically marinated in shōyu, oil, chili peppers, green onions and seaweed. On a hot day, nothing beats a mound of snowy shave ice, packed into a cup and drenched with sweet syrups in an eye-popping rainbow of hues.

Eating Out

Informal dining is Hawaii's forte. For local food and rock-bottom prices, swing by retro drive-ins and diners, open from morning till night. Portion sizes can be gigantic, so feel free to split a meal or take home leftovers, like locals do. For gourmet cuisine by Hawaii's star chefs, explore Honolulu and our recommendations. Open from pau hana (happy hour) until late, most bars serve tasty pupu (appetizers or small shared plates) like poke, shrimp tempura or edamame (fresh soybeans in the pod). The casual Hawaii dress code means T-shirts and flip-flops are ubiquitous, except at Honolulu's most upscale restaurants and at Waikiki's luxury resort hotels.

Hawaii-grown fruits and vegetables, fresh seafood and, frankly, magic. Inside an art gallery, bar seats ring the open kitchen. Ceramic turtles hide savory custard in their shells and pottery bowls harbor tea-soaked rice topped with delicately poached fish. Reservations essential. (☎ 808-521-0141; www. guiloguilo.com; 560 Pensacola St; chef's tasting menu $50-60; ☺ 6pm-midnight Thu-Mon)

Entertainment

Republik   LIVE MUSIC

11 ⭐ Map p50, D4

Honolulu's most intimate concert hall for touring and local acts – indie rockers, punk and metal bands, and more – has a graffiti-bomb vibe and backlit black walls that trippily light up. Buy tickets for shows in advance, to make sure you get in and also to save a few bucks. (☎ 808-941-7469; http://jointherepublik.com; 1349 Kapi'olani Blvd; ☺ lounge 6pm-2am Mon-Sat, concert schedules vary)

Jazz Minds Art & Café   LIVE MUSIC

12 ⭐ Map p50, F4

Don't let the nearby strip clubs turn you off this place. This tattered brick-walled lounge with an almost speakeasy ambience pulls in the top island talent – fusion jazz, funk, bebop, hip hop, surf rock and minimalist acts. However, you will need to be prepared for a stiff two-drink minimum. (☎ 808-945-0800; www.honolulujazzclub.com; 1661 Kapi'olani Blvd; cover charge $10; ☺ 9pm-2am Mon-Sat)

Doris Duke Theatre   CINEMA

13 ⭐ Map p50, C1

Shows a mind-bending array of experimental, alternative, retro-classic and art-house films, especially groundbreaking documentaries, inside the Honolulu Museum of Art. For weekday matinees, validated parking costs $3 (evenings and weekends free). (☎ 808-532-8768; www.honolulumuseum.org; Honolulu Museum of Art, 900 S Beretania St; tickets $10)

Ala Moana Centertainment   PERFORMING ARTS

14 ⭐ Map p50, E4

The mega shopping center's courtyard area is the venue for all sorts of island entertainment, including music by O'ahu musicians and the Royal Hawaiian Band, Japanese *taiko* drumming and Sunday-afternoon *keiki* (children's) hula shows also take place. (☎ 808-955-9517; www.alamoanacenter.com; ground fl, Center Court, 1450 Ala Moana Blvd; admission free;)

HawaiiSlam   PERFORMING ARTS

15 ⭐ Map p50, A2

One of the USA's biggest poetry slams, here international wordsmiths, artists, musicians, MCs and DJs share the stage. (www.hawaiislam.com; Fresh Cafe, 831 Queen St; admission before/after 8:30pm $3/5; ☺ 8:30pm 1st Thu of each month)

Shopping

Ward Warehouse   MALL

16 🔒 Map p50, A3

Across the street from Ala Moana Beach, this mini-mall has many

Ala Moana Shopping Center (p49)

one-of-a-kind island shops and eateries. There's a threat that it will all be bowled over to make way for glitzy towers, but at the time of research, Ward Warehouse survives! (www.wardcenters.com; 1050 Ala Moana Blvd; ☺10am-9pm Mon-Sat, to 6pm Sun)

Island Slipper
SHOES

 17 🔒 Map p50, A3

Across Honolulu and Waikiki, scores of stores sell flip-flops (aka 'rubbah slippah'), but nobody else carries such ultracomfy suede and leather styles – all made in Hawaii since 1946 – let alone such giant sizes (as one clerk told us, 'We fit *all* the island people.'). Try on as many pairs as you like until your feet really feel the aloha. (www.island slipper.com; Ward Warehouse, 1050 Ala Moana Blvd; ☺10am-9pm Mon-Sat, to 8pm Sun)

Manuheali'i
CLOTHING

18 🔒 Map p50, G3

Look to this island-born shop for original and modern designs. Hawaiian musicians often sport Manuheali'i's bold-print silk aloha shirts. Flowing synthetic print and knit dresses and wrap tops take inspiration from the traditional muumuu but are transformed into spritely contemporary looks. Also in Kailua. (📞808-942-9868; www.manuhealii.com; 930 Punahou St; ☺9:30am-6pm Mon-Fri, 9am-4pm Sat, 10am-3pm Sun)

Local Life
Stroll Like a UH Student

Getting There

🚌 From Waikiki or downtown Honolulu, take bus 4; from Ala Moana, catch bus 6 or 18.

Only a couple of miles northeast of Waikiki in the foothills of the Manoa Valley, the main campus of the statewide university system, known as UH, is breezy, tree-shaded, and crowded with students from the mainland and islands throughout the Pacific. The campus and surrounding area feel youthful, with a collection of cafes, eclectic restaurants and one-of-a-kind shops.

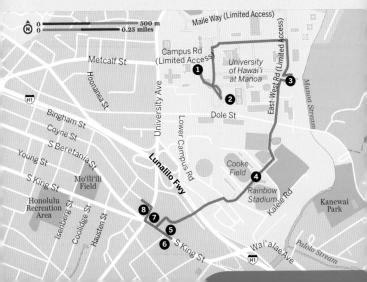

❶ UH Campus Center

Start your stroll at the **UH Campus Center**. The UH Bookstore is here, as are banks, ATMs, coffee shops and a food court. There are crowds of students during the day, but it's almost deserted by evening. Free one-hour walking tours of campus depart here at 2pm Mondays, Wednesdays and Fridays.

❷ John Young Museum of Art

A short walk downhill from the Campus Center, the **John Young Museum of Art** (☎808-956-3634; www.outreach. hawaii.edu/jymuseum; Krauss Hall, 2500 Dole St; admission free; ⏰11am-2pm Mon-Fri, 1-4pm Sun) features 20th-century Hawaii painter Young's collection of artifacts from the Pacific islands, Africa and Asia, mostly ceramics, pottery and sculpture. Although it's not huge, it's worth a quick visit.

❸ East-West Center

Walk the tree-lined McCarthy Mall over to East-West Rd. The **East-West Center** (☎808-944-7111; www.eastwestcenter. org; 1601 East-West Rd) aims to promote mutual understanding among the peoples of Asia, the Pacific and the US. Changing exhibitions of art and culture are displayed in the EWC Gallery. Eye off the **Japanese teahouse** garden and royal **Thai pavilion** outside.

❹ UH Sports Grounds

Head down East-West Rd, cross Dole St and carry on to a staircase down to the **UH sports grounds**. Pass the **tennis courts** and **softball stadium** on your right, then pass behind the **baseball stadium**. When you hit Lower Campus Rd, turn right, then

first left under the freeway and follow your nose out to King St.

❺ Glazers Coffee

It's coffee time and they're serious about their brews at **Glazers Coffee** (☎808-391-6548; www.glazerscoffee.com; 2700 S King St; ⏰7am-11pm Mon-Thu, 7am-9pm Fri, 8am-11pm Sat & Sun; 🛜), a students' hangout where you can kick back on comfy living-room sofas next to jazzy artwork and plentiful electrical outlets.

❻ Kokua Market Natural Foods

Just over on the other side of King St, **Kokua Market Natural Foods** (☎808-941-1922; www.kokua.coop; 2643 S King St; ⏰8am-9pm; 🍴), Hawaii's only natural food co-op, has an organic hot-and-cold salad bar and a vegetarian- and vegan-friendly deli for takeout meals. A great spot to browse and see what's on offer.

❼ Tropics Tap House

Relive your college days at **Tropics Tap House** (☎808-955-5088; www.tropicstap house.com; 1019 University Ave; ⏰2pm-2am Mon-Fri, 11am-2pm Sat & Sun), an open air sports bar on University that couldn't be called fancy, but gets the job done. Standard bar fare, but lots of beers to choose from and even beer cocktails. Lots of big screens for sports.

❽ Bubbies

It would be very hard to pass over **Bubbies** (www.bubbiesicecream.com; Varsity Center, 1010 University Ave; items $1.50-6; ⏰noon-midnight Mon-Thu, to 1am Fri & Sat, to 11:30pm Sun; 🚻), a student favorite to finish your stroll. We're talking bite-sized frozen *mochi* ice-cream treats. The mango *mochi* ice-cream rocks!

Top Sights
Bishop Museum

Getting There

🚌 From Waikiki, take the route 2 ('School St-Middle St') to the intersection of School St and Kapalama Ave.

🚗 Take eastbound H-1 Fwy exit 20 and follow the signs.

Like Hawaii's version of the Smithsonian Institute in Washington, DC, the Bishop Museum showcases a remarkable array of cultural and natural history exhibits. It is often ranked as the finest Polynesian anthropological museum in the world. Founded in 1889 in honor of Princess Bernice Pauahi Bishop, a descendant of the Kamehameha dynasty, it originally housed only Hawaiian and royal artifacts. These days it honors all of Polynesia.

Kahili Room, Bishop Museum

Don't Miss

The Hawaiian Hall

The Hawaiian Hall, residing inside a dignified three-story Victorian building, has displays covering the cultural history of Hawaii. Don't miss the feathered cloak once worn by Kamehameha the Great, created entirely of the yellow feathers of the now-extinct *mamo* – some 80,000 birds were caught and plucked to create this single adornment.

The Polynesian Hall

The fascinating two-story exhibits inside the Polynesian Hall cover the myriad cultures of Polynesia, Micronesia and Melanesia. You could spend hours gazing at astounding and rare ritual artifacts, from elaborate dance masks and ceremonial costumes to carved canoes.

Science Adventure Center

Across the Great Lawn, the eye-popping, state-of-the-art multisensory Science Adventure Center lets kids walk through an erupting volcano, take a mini-submarine dive and play with three floors of interactive multimedia exhibits.

Planetarium

The Bishop Museum is home to O'ahu's only planetarium, which highlights traditional Polynesian methods of wayfaring (navigation), using wave patterns and the position of the stars to travel thousands of miles across the open ocean in traditional outrigger canoes. Shows usually start at 11:30am, 1:30pm and 3:30pm daily except Tuesday, and are included in the museum admission price.

📞 808-847-3511

www.bishopmuseum.org

1525 Bernice St

adult/child $20/15

🕐 9am-5pm Wed-Mon

P 🔗

☑ Top Tips

▶ Check the museum website for special events, including popular 'Moonlight Mele' summer concerts, family-friendly Hawaiian cultural festivities and after-dark planetarium shows (buy tickets online or make reservations by calling 808-848-4168).

▶ A gift shop off the main lobby sells books on the Pacific not easily found elsewhere, as well as some high-quality Hawaiian art, crafts and souvenirs.

✕ Take a Break

It's only a few blocks walk, and well worth the effort, to get to Helena's Hawaiian Food (p133), one of our top-ranked Honolulu eating options.

Top Sights
Lyon Arboretum
& Upper Manoa Valley

Getting There

🚌 From Ala Moana Center or UH, catch bus 5 to the last stop. Walk from there.

🚗 Drive up University Ave past UH, then right on East Manoa Rd.

Oʻahu has lots more to offer that just sand, sun and sea. Take a look inland from Honolulu and Waikiki and you'll see the lush, windy Koʻolau range of mountains, often enshrouded in rain or mist, always covered in green tropical vegetation, and criss-crossed by a myriad of hiking trails. If you head up past the University of Hawaiʻi at Manoa (UH) to the end of the road, you'll find a couple of attractions that will be a pleasant surprise.

Lyon Arboretum

Don't Miss

Lyon Arboretum

Beautifully unkempt walking trails wind through this highly regarded 200-acre arboretum managed by the University of Hawai'i. It was originally founded in 1918 by a group of sugar planters who grew native and exotic flora species to restore Honolulu's watershed and test their economic benefit. This is not your typical overly manicured tropical flower garden, but a mature and largely wooded arboretum, where related species cluster in a semi-natural state.

Manoa Falls Trail

Honolulu's most rewarding short hike, this 1.6-mile round-trip trail runs above a rocky streambed before ending at a pretty little cascade. Tall tree trunks line the often muddy and slippery path. Wild orchids and red ginger grow near the falls, which drop about 100ft into a small, shallow pool. It's illegal to venture beyond the established viewing area.

Nu'uanu Valley Lookout

For a longer, tougher hike, just before Manoa Falls, the marked 'Aihualama Trail heads up to the left, offering broad views of Manoa Valley. It eventually intersects with the Pauoa Flats Trail, which ascends to the spectacular Nu'uanu Valley Lookout. High atop the Ko'olau Range, it's possible to peer through a gap over to the Windward Coast. The total round-trip distance to the lookout from the Manoa Falls trailhead is approximately 5.5 miles.

📞 info 808-988-0456, tour reservations 808-988-0461

www.hawaii.edu/lyonarboretum

3860 Manoa Rd

donation $5, guided tour $10

🕐 8am-4pm Mon-Fri, 9am-3pm Sat, tours usually 10am Mon-Fri P ♿

☑ Top Tips

▶ Even if you are sitting in sunshine in Waikiki, look inland before you head up the Manoa Valley – it may be pouring with rain inland.

▶ If you've got a car, pick up a picnic lunch at Andy's Sandwiches on your way up the valley.

▶ It can get hot and mosquitoes can be a nuisance. Come prepared with insect repellant, a hat, sunscreen and liquids.

✕ Take a Break

Andy's Sandwiches (📞 808-988-6161; www.andyssandwiches.com; 2904 E Manoa Rd; items $4-12; 🕐 7am-5pm Mon-Thu, to 4pm Fri, to 2.30pm Sun) makes up great salads and sandwiches, while the **Wai'oli Tea Room** (📞 808-988-5800; www.thewaiolitearoom.com; 2950 Manoa Rd; 🕐 8am-2pm) has tasty lunch options.

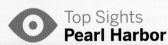

Top Sights
Pearl Harbor

Getting There

🚌 From Waikiki take bus 42 to the Arizona Memorial stop (1 hour).

🚗 From Honolulu or Waikiki, take H-1 west to exit 15A (Arizona Memorial/Stadium), then follow the signs.

The WWII-era rallying cry 'Remember Pearl Harbor!', once mobilizing an entire nation, dramatically resonates on O'ahu. It was here that the surprise Japanese attack on December 7, 1941 – 'a date which will live in infamy,' President Franklin D Roosevelt later said – hurtled the US into war in the Pacific. Every year about 1.6 million tourists visit Pearl Harbor's unique collection of war memorials and museums, all clustered around a quiet bay where oysters were once farmed.

Aerial view of Pearl Harbor

Don't Miss

WWII Valor in the Pacific National Monument

One of the USA's most significant WWII sites, this National Park Service monument narrates the history of the Pearl Harbor attack and commemorates fallen service members. The main entrance also leads to Pearl Harbor's other parks and museums.

The monument grounds include two museums, the Road to War and the Attack & Aftermath, where multimedia and interactive displays bring the facts to life through historic photos, films, illustrated graphics and taped oral histories. A shore-side walk passes signs illustrating how the attack unfolded in the now-peaceful harbor.

USS Arizona Memorial

This somber monument commemorates the Pearl Harbor attack and its fallen service members with an offshore shrine reachable by boat. The USS Arizona Memorial was built over the midsection of the sunken USS *Arizona,* with deliberate geometry to represent initial defeat, ultimate victory and eternal serenity. In the furthest of three chambers inside the shrine, the names of crewmen killed in the attack are engraved onto a marble wall. In its rush to recover from the attack and prepare for war, the US Navy exercised its option to leave the servicemen inside the sunken ship; they remain entombed in its hull, buried at sea. Visitors are asked to maintain respectful silence at all times.

Battleship Missouri Memorial

The last battleship built at the end of WWII, the USS *Missouri* provides a unique historical 'bookend' to the US campaign in the Pacific.

www.nps.gov/valr/

admission free, Passport to Pearl Harbor 7-days adult/ child $65/35

☑ Top Tips

▶ Strict security measures are in place at Pearl Harbor. You are not allowed to bring in any items that allow concealment (eg purses, camera bags, fanny packs, backpacks, diaper bags). Personal-sized cameras and camcorders are allowed.

▶ Don't lock valuables in your car. Instead use the storage facility outside the main park gate.

▶ Book tickets online and early.

✖ Take a Break

All four sights have concession stands or snack shops. The cafe at the Pacific Aviation Museum is the biggest, with the best selection; the hot dogs at Bowfin Park are the cheapest.

Understand
The Pearl Harbor Attack

December 7, 1941, began at 7:55am with a wave of more than 350 Japanese planes swooping over the Koʻolau Range headed toward the unsuspecting US Pacific Fleet in Pearl Harbor. The battleship USS *Arizona* took a direct hit and sank in less than nine minutes, trapping most of its crew beneath the surface. The average age of the 1177 enlisted men who died in the attack on the ship was just 19 years. It wasn't until 15 minutes after the bombing started that American anti-aircraft guns began to shoot back at the Japanese warplanes. Twenty other US military ships were sunk or seriously damaged and 347 airplanes were destroyed during the two-hour attack.

Nicknamed the 'Mighty Mo' this decommissioned battleship saw action during the decisive WWII battles of Iwo Jima and Okinawa.

The USS *Missouri* is now docked on Ford Island, just a few hundred yards from the sunken remains of the USS *Arizona*. During a self-guided audio tour, you can poke about the officers'

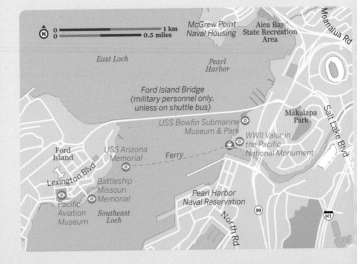

USS Arizona Memorial (p65)

USS Oklahoma Memorial, Ford Island

quarters, browse exhibits on the ship's history and stride across the deck where General MacArthur accepted the Japanese surrender on September 2, 1945.

USS Bowfin Submarine Museum & Park

This park harbors the moored WWII-era submarine USS *Bowfin* and a museum that traces the development of submarines from their origins to the nuclear age, including wartime patrol footage. Undoubtedly, the highlight is clambering aboard a historic subma-

rine. Launched on December 7, 1942, one year after the Pearl Harbor attack, the USS *Bowfin* sank 44 enemy ships in the Pacific by the end of WWII.

Pacific Aviation Museum

This military aircraft museum covers WWII through the US conflicts in Korea and Vietnam. The first aircraft hangar has been outfitted with exhibits on the Pearl Harbor attack, the Doolittle Raid on mainland Japan in 1942 and the pivotal Battle of Midway, when the tides of WWII in the Pacific turned in favor of the Allies.

Explore

Waikiki

Waikiki – the name alone will have you thinking of boundless horizons, Pacific sunsets and hula dancers gently swaying to the beat of island rhythms. Once the playground of Hawaiian royalty, this remains O'ahu's quintessential beach. And Waikiki has reinvented itself, moving beyond plastic mass tourism, with stylish resort hotels, fashion-forward boutiques, and sophisticated restaurants and cocktail lounges.

The Sights in a Day

Start your day admiring the **King David Kalakaua Statue** (p78) on Kalakaua Ave, then have breakfast at **Eggs 'n' Things** (p82). Head to the **Hawai'i Army Museum** (p80) for a completely different look at Waikiki. You're out onto **Fort DeRussy Beach** (p76) from there.

Wander along the beachfront, then head through the Sheraton Waikiki to the historic **Royal Hawaiian Hotel** (p79). A bit further down the street, head into the **Moana Surfrider Hotel** (p79) then back out to the beach. Check out the **Wizard Stones of Kapaemahu** (p78), the **Duke Kahanamoku Statue** (p89) and if time is on your side, stroll down through **Kapi'olani Beach Park** (p77) to **Waikiki Aquarium** (p79).

It must be drinks time by now! Head back to **Kuhio Beach** (p70) for a sunset cruise on the **Na Hoku II** (p78), complete with open bar. For dinner, grab a cab to **Uncle Bo's** (p133) on Kapahulu Ave, and if you can squeeze any more in, head up to **Leonard's** (p133) for *malasadas* for dessert.

For a local's day in Waikiki, see p72.

 Top Sights

Kuhio Beach (p70)

Local Life

A Wander Through Waikiki (p72)

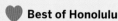 **Best of Honolulu**

Eating
Rainbow Drive-in (p73)

Uncle Bo's Pupu Bar & Grill (p133)

Leonard's (p133)

Drinking & Entertainment
RumFire (p84)

House Without a Key (p88)

Mai Tai Bar (p88)

'Aha 'Aina (p90)

Hawaiiana Shopping
Bailey's Antiques & Aloha Shirts (p73)

Na Lima Mili Hulu No'eau (p92)

Ukulele PuaPua (p92)

For Kids
Waikiki Aquarium (p79)

Honolulu Zoo (p80)

Getting There

🚌 **Bus** Most public bus stops are inland on Kuhio Ave. Buses head all over.

🚗 **Car** To get to Waikiki from the airport or downtown, take either The H-1 (Lunalilo Fwy), or Hwy 92 (Nimitz Hwy/Ala Moana Blvd). Parking is expensive.

Top Sights
Kuhio Beach

Let's face it, chances are that this is what you're here for – a bit of excitement and fun in the sun! If you're the kind of person who wants it all, Kuhio Beach offers everything from protected swimming to outrigger-canoe or catamaran rides to your first time on a surfboard, and even a free sunset-hula and Hawaiian-music show. This is where it's at, and it's all likely to be within a short stagger of your hotel room.

👁 Map p74, E4

Rental watercraft, Kuhio Beach

Don't Miss

Duke's Statue

On the waterfront on Kalakaua Ave, this wonderful statue of Duke Kahanamoku is always draped in colorful lei. Duke was a real Hawaiian hero, winning numerous Olympic swimming medals and becoming known as 'the father of modern surfing.' He even had stints as Sheriff of Honolulu and as a Hollywood actor.

Torch Lighting & Hula Show

It all begins at the Duke Kahanamoku statue with the sounding of a conch shell and the lighting of torches after sunset. At the nearby hula mound, lay out your beach towel and enjoy the authentic Hawaiian music and dance show. It's on Tuesday, Thursday and Saturday evenings, free and full of aloha!

Kapahulu Groin

Kapahulu Groin is a walled storm drain with a walkway on top that juts out into the ocean and is one of Waikiki's hottest bodyboarding spots. If the surf's right, you can find a few dozen bodyboarders riding the waves. These experienced locals ride straight for the groin's cement wall and then veer away at the last moment, thrilling the tourists watching them from the little pier above.

Prince Kuhio Statue

This statue celebrates the man who was prince of the reigning House of Kalakaua when the Kingdom of Hawaii was overthrown in 1893. When Hawaii was annexed as a territory of the United States, Kuhio was elected as Hawaii's congressional delegate for 10 consecutive terms. The beach is named after him and the statue is often draped in lei.

☑ **Top Tips**

▶ You'll find restrooms, outdoor showers, a snack bar, surfboard lockers and beach-gear-rental stands at Waikiki Beach Center, near the friendly police substation.

▶ Those not confident in the water should head for Kapahulu Groin, at the Diamond Head end of Kuhio Beach. A low stone breakwater, called the Wall, runs out from Kapahulu Groin, parallel to the beach. It was built to control sand erosion and, in the process, two nearly enclosed swimming pools were formed.

▶ Ubiquitous **ABC stores** on Kalakaua Ave sell everything you could need to enhance your day – drinks and snacks, sunhats, sunscreen, snorkel sets, T-shirts and, of course, dashboard hula dolls.

✕ **Take a Break**

Head across Kalakaua Ave to LuLu's Surf Club (p83) for liquid refreshments at Happy Hour (3pm to 5pm).

Local Life
A Wander Through Waikiki

Waikiki may be full of tourists, but don't forget that the locals live here, too. From the southern end of Kuhio Beach Park, Kalakaua Ave heads south through Kapi'olani Park; Monsarrat Ave runs between the zoo and the park, past Waikiki School (lucky kids!) and up to Diamond Head; Kapahulu Ave heads east past Waikiki-Kapahulu Library up towards the university.

1 Surfer on a Wave Statue

Start your walk at Kapahulu Groin, the walkway heading out into the ocean at the southern end of Kuhio Beach. Across the road is the zoo entrance, Queen's Surf Beach is right there, as is the Surfer on a Wave statue that celebrates surfing as a major part of the culture of Waikiki.

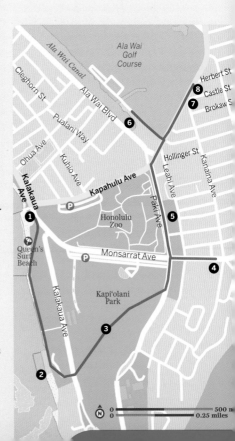

➋ Kaimana Beach

Wander south along the beachfront of Kapi'olani Beach Park. This quiet stretch, backed by banyan trees and grassy lawns is popular with local families, especially on weekends. At the Diamond Head edge of Waikiki you'll find Sans Souci Beach (known to locals as Kaimana Beach), a lovely spot for a swim and a break.

➌ Kapi'olani Park

Head over Kapahulu Ave and into Kapi'olani Park, named after Queen Kapi'olani, the wife of King David Kalakaua – his statue at the other end of Waikiki greets visitors to Waikiki. This massive park is a beloved outdoor venue for live music and local community gatherings, from farmers markets to arts-and-crafts fairs to festivals to rugby matches.

➍ Diamond Head Cove Health Bar

Over on Monsarrat Ave, turn right and walk up past Waikiki School. In the small strip-mall beyond the school you'll find **Diamond Head Cove Health Bar** (www.diamondheadcove.com; 3045 Monsarrat Ave, Ste 5; ⏰10am-8pm Mon & Sat, 9am-11pm Tue-Thu, 9am-8pm Fri, 10am-11pm Sun), specializing in refreshing acai bowls, fruit smoothies, healthy wraps, fresh *poke* and sashimi.

➎ Paki Community Park

Wander down leafy Paki Ave, past Paki Community Park, a locals hangout with surprisingly good games of pick-up basketball going on. There's a small community center, a children's playground, and if you look carefully, you may spot the giraffes over the road in Honolulu Zoo. Turn right when you reach Kapahulu Ave.

➏ Ala Wai Canal

Down the road next to Waikiki-Kapahulu Public Library you'll find **Ala Wai Golf Course** (☎reservations 808-296-2000; www.honolulu.gov/des/golf/alawai. html; 404 Kapahulu Ave; green fees $22-55) and Ala Wai Canal, created in 1922 to drain the rice paddies, marshes and swamps that would become present-day Waikiki. It's a popular spot with kayakers and outrigger-canoe teams.

➐ Rainbow Drive-in

Must be time for a break and you can't get more local than **Rainbow Drive-in** (☎808-737-0177; www.rainbowdrivein.com; 3308 Kanaina Ave; meals $4-9; ⏰7am-9pm; 🍴). Started by an island-born US Army cook after WWII, this classic Hawaii drive-in wrapped in rainbow-colored neon is a throwback to another era. Factoid: President Barack Obama eats here.

➑ Bailey's Antiques & Aloha Shirts

Without a doubt, **Bailey's** (http://aloha shirts.com; 517 Kapahulu Ave; ⏰10am-6pm) has the finest aloha-shirt collection on O'ahu, possibly the world! Racks are crammed with thousands of aloha shirts with prices varying from five bucks to several thousand dollars. 'Margaritaville' musician Jimmy Buffett is Bailey's biggest fan.

A

Holomoana St
27
92
Ala Moana Blvd

B

Rainbow Dr
33
37
Kalia Rd
Paoa Pl
Maluhia Rd

C

King David
Kalakaua
Statue
8
Kuano'o St
Namahana St
Olohana St
Kalakaua Ave

D

Ala Wai Blvd
Ala Wai
Park
Kalaimoku St
Launiu St
Kuhio Ave
Ka'iolu St

1

Ala Wai
Yacht
Harbor
P

Hilton
Lagoon

1
Kahanamoku
Beach

2

Fort
DeRussy
Beach
2

Fort DeRussy
Military
Reservation

WAIKIKI

Storyteller Statue
15
24
23
Laulula St
Saratoga Rd
Beach Walk
Lewers St

22
Lewers St
Aloha Dr
Manukai St
Waikolulani Ave
Royal Hawaiian Way
Seaside Ave
40

Hawai'i
Army
Museum
14
35

26
Helumoa Rd
28
29
32

38
39
36
Duke's La
Kalakaua Ave
P

3
Gray's
Beach

11
Royal
Hawaiian
Hotel

3

Kahaloa
& Ulukou
Beaches
4

4

Mamala Bay

5

E   F   G   H

Olu St

Mokihana St

Paliuli St

Kapahulu Ave

Winam Ave

Manoa-Palolo Drainage Canal

Date St

Palani Ave

Ala Wai Canal

Ala Wai
Golf Course

41 🔒 Hunter St
42 🔒 Williams St

Mooheau Ave

Hoolulu St

Nohonani St
Nahua St

30 17 31
21   Walina St

16   Kanekapolei St

Ka'iulani Ave

Cleghorn St

Ala Wai Blvd

Herbert St

Castle St   Campbell Ave

Brokaw St

Moana
Surfrider
Hotel

12

Koa Ave

Kuhio Ave

Uluniu Ave

20
19
18

Lili'uokalani Ave

Pualani Way

Wai Nani Way

'Ainakea Way

Hollinger St

Kanaina Ave

7   Wizard Stones
of Kapaemahu

Kealohilani Ave

Kuhio
Beach

Ohua Ave

Pa'oakalani Ave

34

Kapahulu Ave

Leahi Ave

Paki Ave

Kapahulu
Groin

25   Cartwright Rd
Lemon Rd

Kuhio Ave

Honolulu Zoo

13   Honolulu
Zoo

Honolulu
Zoo

P

Queen's
Surf Beach

7

43

Queen Kapi'olani
Statue

Kapi'olani
Park

Monsarrat Ave

9

P

5 6   10

Kalakaua Ave

0 —————————— 500 m
0 —————————— 0.25 miles

Sights

Kahanamoku Beach   BEACH

1 ◎ Map p74, A2

Fronting the Hilton Hawaiian Village, Kahanamoku Beach is Waikiki's westernmost beach. It takes its name from Duke Kahanamoku (1890–1968), the legendary Waikiki beachboy whose family once owned the land where the resort now stands. Hawaii's champion surfer and Olympic gold medal winner learned to swim here. The beach offers calm swimming conditions and a gently sloping, if rocky, bottom. Public access is at the end of Paoa Pl, off Kalia Rd.

Fort DeRussy Beach   BEACH

2 ◎ Map p74, B2

Seldom crowded, this often-overlooked beauty extends along the shore of a military reservation. Like all beaches in Hawaii, it's free and open to the public. The water is usually calm and good for swimming, but it's shallow at low tide. When conditions are right, windsurfers, bodyboarders and board surfers all play here. Usually open daily, beach-hut concessionaires rent bodyboards, kayaks and snorkel sets. A grassy lawn with palm trees offers some sparse shade, an alternative to frying on the sand. (♿)

Gray's Beach   BEACH

3 ◎ Map p74, C3

Nestled up against the Halekulani luxury resort, Gray's Beach has suffered some of the Waikiki strip's worst erosion. Because the seawall in front of the Halekulani hotel is so close to the waterline, the beach sand fronting the hotel is often totally submerged

---

Understand
Waikiki Beach's Many Faces

The 2-mile stretch of white sand that everyone calls Waikiki Beach runs from Hilton Hawaiian Village all the way to Kapi'olani Beach Park. Along the way, the beach keeps changing names and personalities. In the early morning, quiet seaside paths belong to walkers and runners, and strolling toward Diamond Head at dawn can be a meditative experience. By mid-morning it looks like any resort beach – packed with watersports concessionaires and lots of tourist bodies. By noon it's a challenge to walk along the packed beach without stepping on anyone.

Waikiki is good for swimming, bodyboarding, surfing, sailing and other water sports most of the year, and there are lifeguards, restrooms and outdoor showers scattered along the beachfront. Between May and September, summer swells make the water a little rough for swimming, but great for surfing. For snorkeling, head to Sans Souci Beach Park or Queen's Surf Beach.

ANN CECIL / GETTY IMAGES ©

Fort DeRussy Beach

by the surf, but the offshore waters are shallow and calm, offering decent swimming conditions. Public access is along a paved walkway. It was named after Gray's-by-the-Sea, a 1920s boarding house that stood here.

Kahaloa & Ulukou Beaches

BEACH

4 ⊙ Map p74, D3

The beach between the Royal Hawaiian and Moana Surfrider hotels is Waikiki's busiest section of sand and surf, great for sunbathing, swimming and people-watching. Most of the beach has a shallow bottom with a gradual slope. The only drawback for swimmers is its popularity with beginning surfers, and the occasional catamaran landing hazard. Queens and Canoes, Waikiki's best-known surf breaks, are just offshore. Paddle further offshore over a lagoon to Populars (aka 'Pops'), a favorite of long-boarders.

Kapi'olani Beach Park

BEACH

5 ⊙ Map p74, F5

Where did all the tourists go? From Kapahulu Groin south to the Natatorium, this peaceful stretch of beach, backed by a green space of banyan trees and grassy lawns, offers a relaxing niche with none of the frenzy found on the beaches fronting the Waikiki hotel strip. Facilities include restrooms and outdoor showers.

Top Tip

Sail Away!

Several catamaran cruises leave right from Waikiki Beach – just walk down to the sand, step into the surf and hop aboard. A 90-minute, all-you-can-drink 'booze cruise' will typically cost you $25 to $40 per adult. Reservations are recommended for sunset sails, which sell out fast.

Top choices are **Na Hoku II** (Map p74, D3; 808-554-5990; www.nahokuii.com; incl drinks $30), a catamaran with unmistakable yellow-and-red striped sails that heads out four times daily (every two hours from 11.30am to 5.30pm), and **Maita'i** (Map p74, C3; 808-922-5665; www.leahi.com; adult/child from $28/14;), a similar cat with green sails.

Kapiʻolani Beach is a popular weekend picnicking spot for local families, who unload the kids to splash in the ocean while adults fire up the BBQ.

Sans Souci Beach Park BEACH

6 Map p74, F5

At the Diamond Head edge of Waikiki, Sans Souci is a prime sandy stretch of oceanfront that's far from the frenzied tourist scene. It's commonly called Kaimana Beach, as it's next door to the New Otani Kaimana Beach Hotel. Local residents often come here for their daily swims. A shallow reef close to shore makes for calm, protected waters and provides good snorkeling.

Wizard Stones of Kapaemahu STATUE

7 Map p74, E3

Near the police substation at Waikiki Beach Center, four ordinary-looking boulders are actually the legendary Wizard Stones of Kapaemahu, said to contain the mana (power) of four wizards who came to Oʻahu from Tahiti around 400 AD. According to ancient legend, the wizards helped the island residents by relieving their aches and pains and their fame became widespread. As tribute when the wizards left, the islanders placed the four boulders where the wizards had lived.

King David Kalakaua Statue STATUE

8 Map p74, C1

Born in 1836, King Kalakaua ruled Hawaii from 1874 until his death in 1891. With his wife, Queen Kapiʻolani, Kalakaua traveled the world extensively. This statue, designed by Native Hawaiian sculptor Sean Browne, greets visitors coming into Waikiki and was donated by the Japanese-American Community of Hawaii to mark 100 years of Japanese immigration in 1985. Kalakaua was instrumental in the signing of a Japan-Hawaii Labor Convention that brought 200,000 Japanese immigrants to Hawaii between 1885 and 1924.

Queen Kapiʻolani Statue STATUE

9 Map p74, F5

This bronze statue depicts Queen Kapiʻolani, the wife of King David

Kalakaua. The Queen was a beloved philanthropist, known as the queen who loved children. Among other accomplishments, she founded a maternity home in 1890 for disadvantaged Hawaiians and today you'll hear her name often – the park, a hospital, a major boulevard and a community college are named for her.

Waikiki Aquarium
AQUARIUM

10 ◉ Map p74, F5

Located on Waikiki's shoreline, this university-run aquarium features dozens of tanks that re-create diverse tropical Pacific reef habitats. Check the website or call ahead to make reservations for special family-friendly events and fun educational programs for kids such as Aquarium After Dark adventures. It's about a 15-minute walk southeast of the main Waikiki beach strip. (☎808-923-9741; www.waquarium.org; 2777 Kalakaua Ave; adult/child $12/5; ☺9am-5pm, last entry 4:30pm; ☝)

Royal Hawaiian Hotel
HISTORIC BUILDING

11 ◉ Map p74, D3

With its Moorish-style turrets and archways, this gorgeously restored 1927 art-deco landmark, dubbed the 'Pink Palace,' is a throwback to the era when Rudolph Valentino was *the* romantic idol and travel to Hawaii was by Matson Navigation luxury liner. Its guest list read like a who's-who of A-list celebrities, from royalty to Rockefellers,

along with luminaries such as Charlie Chaplin and Babe Ruth. Today, historic tours explore the architecture and lore of this grande dame. (☎808-923-7311; www.royal-hawaiian.com; 2259 Kalakaua Ave; admission free; ☺tours 2pm Tue & Thu)

Moana Surfrider Hotel
HISTORIC BUILDING

12 ◉ Map p74, E3

Christened the Moana Hotel when it opened in 1901, this beaux-arts plantation-style inn was once the haunt of Hollywood movie stars, aristocrats and business tycoons. The historic hotel embraces a seaside courtyard with a big banyan tree and a wraparound veranda, where island musicians and hula dancers perform in the evenings. (☎808-922-3111; www.moana-surfrider.com; 2365 Kalakaua Ave; admission free; ☺tours 11am Mon, Wed & Fri)

Top Tip

Need Snorkel Gear?

A top spot to get your rental gear is **Snorkel Bob's** (Map p75, H2; 📞808-735-7944; www.snorkelbob.com; 702 Kapahulu Ave; ☺8am-5pm). Rates vary depending on the quality of the snorkeling gear and accessories packages, but excellent weekly discounts are available and online reservations taken. You can even rent gear on O'ahu, then return it on another island.

Honolulu Zoo   ZOO

 13 Map p74, F5

Honolulu Zoo does a great job on limited finances of showcasing tropical animals from around the globe. There are 40-plus acres of tropical greenery, animals and a petting zoo for kids. Hawaii has no endemic land mammals, but in the aviary near the entrance you can see some native birds, including the *nene* (Hawaiian goose) and *'apapane,* a bright-red Hawaiian honeycreeper. Make reservations for family-oriented twilight tours, dinner safaris, zoo campouts and stargazing nights. (📞808-971-7171; www.honoluluzoo.org; cnr Kapahulu & Kalakaua Aves; adult/child 4-12yr $14/6; ☺9am-4:30pm; 🅿🚻)

Hawai'i Army Museum   MUSEUM

14 Map p74, C2

At Fort DeRussy, this museum showcases an almost mind-numbing array of military paraphernalia as it relates to Hawaii's history, starting with shark-tooth clubs that Kamehameha the Great used to win control of the island more than two centuries ago. Fascinating old photographs and stories help bring an understanding of the influence of the US military presence in Hawaii. (www.hiarmymuseumsoc.org; 2161 Kalia Rd; donations welcome, audiotour $5; ☺9am-5pm Tue-Sat, last entry 4:45pm; 🅿)

Storyteller Statue   STATUE

 15 Map p74, C2

This bronze statue just off Kalakaua Ave represents 'The Storytellers,' the keepers of Hawaiian culture. For centuries, women have been at the top of Hawaiian oral traditions, and the storytellers preserve the identity of their people and land by reciting poems, songs, chants and genealogies. The Storyteller's brother-statue is the Water Giver statue at the Hawaiian Convention Center.

Eating

Food Pantry   SUPERMARKET $

 16 Map p74, E3

It's more expensive than chain supermarkets found elsewhere in Honolulu, but cheaper than buying groceries at Waikiki's convenience stores; look for a Coffee Bean & Tea Leaf coffee bar inside. (2370 Kuhio Ave; ☺6am-1am)

Marukame Udon   JAPANESE $

17 Map p74, E2

Everybody loves this Japanese noodle shop, which is so popular there is

Summer concert at Honolulu Zoo

often a line stretching down the sidewalk. Watch those thick udon noodles get rolled, cut and boiled fresh right in front of you, then stack mini plates of giant tempura and *musubi* (rice balls) stuffed with salmon or a sour plum on your cafeteria tray. (📞808-931-6000; www.facebook.com/marukameudon; 2310 Kuhio Ave; mains $2-8; ⏰7am-9am & 11am-10pm; 🚶)

Ruffage Natural Foods
HEALTH FOOD $

18 ✗ Map p74, E3

This pint-sized health-food store whips up taro burgers, veggie burritos, deli sandwiches with fresh avocado and real-fruit smoothies that will revitalize your whole body. At night, the grocery shop shares space with a tiny, backpacker-friendly sushi bar run by a Japanese expat chef. (📞808-922-2042; www.facebook.com/ruffage.naturalfoods; 2443 Kuhio Ave; mains $4-8; ⏰9am-9pm; 🚶)

Me's BBQ
HAWAIIAN, KOREAN $

19 ✗ Map p74, E3

The street-side takeout counter may be a tad short on atmosphere, but there are plastic tables sitting in the sunshine where you can chow down on Korean standards such as *kimchi* and *kalbi* (marinated short ribs). The wall-size picture menu offers a mind-boggling array of mixed-plate combos including chicken *katsu* (batter-fried chicken), Portuguese sausage and

PHOTO RESOURCE HAWAII / ALAMY ©

eggs, and other only-in-Hawaii tastes. (808-926-9717; 151 Uluniu Ave; mains $5-12; ⏰7am-8:45pm Mon-Sat; 🚼)

Musubi Cafe Iyasume   JAPANESE $

20 Map p74, E3

Hole-in-the-wall keeps busy making fresh *onigiri* (rice balls) stuffed with seaweed, salmon roe, sour plums and even Spam. Other specialties include salmon-roe rice bowls, bizarre Japanese curry and island-style *mochiko* fried chicken. In a hurry? Grab a *bentō* (boxed lunch) to go. (www.tonsuke.com/ eomusubiya.html; 2427 Kuhio Ave, Pacific Monarch Hotel; menu items $2-8; ⏰6:30am-8pm)

Veggie Star Natural Foods   HEALTHY $

21 Map p74, E2

For organic, all-natural and health-conscious groceries, plus tropical smoothies and monster-sized vegetarian burritos, fake-meat burgers, salads and 'airplane ready' sandwiches wrapped to go, visit this little side-street shop. It's the vegan chili that makes the

☑ Top Tip

Workout in Waikiki

For an indoor workout in Waikiki, **24-Hour Fitness** (Map p75, E4; ☎808-923-9090; www.24hourfitness. com; 2490 Kalakaua Ave; daily/weekly pass $25/75; ⏰24hr) is a modern gym with cardio and weight machines and group classes.

most people rave. (808-922-9568; 417 Nahua St; ⏰10am-6pm Mon-Sat; 🚲)

Siam Square   THAI $$

22 Map p74, D2

It's Waikiki's most authentic Thai restaurant, although that's not saying much. You want it spicy? You won't have to work too hard to convince your waitress that you can handle the heat when you order *larb* pork salad or fried fish with chili sauce. Service is standoffish, but the kitchen works so fast and furiously that you probably won't mind. (☎808-923-5320; 2nd fl, 408 Lewers St; mains $11-16; ⏰11am-10.30pm; 🚲)

Ramen Nakamura   JAPANESE $$

23 Map p74, C2

Hit this urban connoisseurs' noodle shop at lunchtime and you'll have to strategically elbow aside Japanese tourists toting Gucci and Chanel bags just to sit down. Then you're free to dig into hearty bowls of oxtail or *tonkatsu* (breaded and fried pork cutlets) or *kimchi* ramen soup with crunchy fried garlic slices on top. Cash only. (☎808-922-7960; 2141 Kalakaua Ave; mains $9-14; ⏰11am-11:30pm)

Eggs 'n' Things   BREAKFAST $$

24 Map p74, C2

Never empty, this bustling diner dishes straight-up comfort food: banana-and-mac-nut pancakes with tropical syrups (guava, honey or coconut), sugary crepes topped with fresh fruit, or fluffy omelets scrambled with Portuguese sausage. You'll fit right in with the early-morning crowd of jet-lagged tourists lined up outside the door – and sometimes around the block. (www.eggsnthings.com; 343 Saratoga Rd; mains $9-18; ⏱6am-2pm & 4-10pm; 👪)

LuLu's Surf Club

AMERICAN $$

25 🍴 Map p74, F4

Surfboards on the wall and an awesome ocean view set the mood at this gregarious open-air restaurant, bar and nightclub. LuLu's filling breakfasts, complete with 'dawn patrol' omelets, eggs Benedict, stuffed French toast, *loco moco* and fruit bowls, are legendary. Sunset Happy Hour runs everyday 3pm to 5pm. (☎808-926-5222; www.luluswaikiki.com; Park Shore Waikiki, 2586 Kalakaua Ave; mains breakfast $6-15, dinner $10-24; ⏱7am-2am; 👪)

Sansei Seafood Restaurant & Sushi Bar

JAPANESE, FUSION $$

From the mind of one of Hawaii's hottest chefs, DK Kodama, this Pacific Rim restaurant (see 34 ⭐ Map p75, F4) rolls out everything from 'new look' fusion sushi and sashimi to Dungeness crab ramen with black-truffle broth – all to rave reviews. Tables on the torch-lit verandah equal prime sunset views. (☎808-931-6286; www.sanseihawaii.com; 3rd fl, Marriott Waikiki Beach Resort, 2552 Kalakaua Ave; most shared plates $5-20, mains $16-35; ⏱5:30-10pm Sun-Thu, to 1am Fri & Sat)

Veranda

CAFE $$$

For colonial atmosphere that harks back to early-20th-century tourist traditions, traditional afternoon tea here (see 12 ◉ Map p75, E3) comes complete with finger sandwiches, scones with pillowy Devonshire cream and tropically flavored pastries. Portions are small, but the oceanfront setting and house-blended teas are memorable. Make reservations and come prepared to shoo away those pesky beggar birds. (☎808-921-4600; www.moana-surfrider.com; Moana Surfrider, 2365 Kalakaua Ave; afternoon tea from $34; ⏱6-11am, midday-3pm; 🅿)

Roy's Waikiki

HAWAII REGIONAL $$$

26 🍴 Map p74, C2

This contemporary incarnation of Roy Yamaguchi's island-born chain is perfect for a flirty date or just celebrating the good life. The ground-breaking chef doesn't actually cook in the kitchen here, but his signature *misoyaki* butterfish, blackened ahi (tunafish) and macadamia-nut-encrusted mahi-mahi are always on the menu (vegans and vegetarians have options, too). Molten-chocolate soufflé for dessert is a must. (☎808-923-7697; www.royshawaii.com; 226 Lewers St; mains $30-60; ⏱11am-9:30pm Mon-Thu, to 10pm Fri-Sun)

Azure

SEAFOOD $$$

Azure is the signature restaurant at the Royal Hawaiian Hotel (see 11 ◉ Map p74, D3). Seafood fresh from the pier,

Top Tip

Hiking Hawaii Cafe & Tours

Hiking Hawaii Cafe (Map p74, B1; 📞855-808-4453; hikinghawaii808.com/cafe.php; 1910 Ala Moana Blvd; ⊘7am-9pm Tue-Sat, to 3pm Sun & Mon; 🛜) is a downstairs eco-cafe serving up healthy meals such as paninis, wraps and smoothies using fresh local produce. There's complimentary wi-fi and the cafe serves as base for Hiking Hawaii's various daily tours on O'ahu. A great spot to hang out.

such as Kona abalone, red snapper and *ono* (white-fleshed mackerel), are all exquisitely prepared island-style, with finishing touches such as red Hawaiian sea salt and Moloka'i purple sweet potatoes on the side. (📞808-921-4600; www.azurewaikiki.com; Royal Hawaiian, 2259 Kalakaua Ave; mains from $38, 5-course tasting menu $79; ⊘5:30-9pm)

Morimoto Waikiki   ASIAN FUSION $$$

27   Map p74, A1

In Modern Honolulu boutique hotel, Iron Chef Morimoto's oceanfront dining room seduces with coconut cocktails and yacht-harbor views from a sunny poolside patio. Sink back against a mod sea-green pillow banquette and fork into cubic seafood *poke* and sushi rolls, ginger-soy braised black cod, wagyu beef *loco moco* or curried whole roasted lobster.

Complimentary valet parking with restaurant validation. (📞808-943-5900; www.morimotowaikiki.com; Modern Honolulu, 1775 Ala Moana Blvd; lunch $18-35, dinner mains $22-50; ⊘11am-2:30pm & 5-10pm; 🅿)

Nobu   JAPANESE, FUSION $$$

28   Map p74, C3

Nobu Matsuhisa's first Japanese-fusion restaurant and sushi bar in Hawaii has made a big splash, and his elegant seafood tapas tastes right at home by the beach. Broiled black cod with miso sauce, new-style sashimi with spicy sauce drizzled on top and Japanese-Peruvian *tiradito* (ceviche) rank among Nobu's signature tastes. A low-lit cocktail lounge serves appetizing small bites and 'sake-tinis.' (📞808-237-6999; www.noburestaurants.com/waikiki; Waikiki Parc, 2233 Helumoa Rd; shared dishes $5-48, mains $30-40; ⊘restaurant 5:30-10pm Sun-Thu, to 10:30pm Fri & Sat, lounge 5pm-midnight daily)

Drinking

RumFire   BAR

The collection of vintage rum is mighty tempting at this lively hotel bar at the Sheraton Waikiki (see 38 🔒 Map p74, D3), with flirty fire pits looking out onto the beach and live contemporary Hawaiian (or jazz) music. Or wander over to the resort's cabana-like Edge of Waikiki Bar for knockout views, designer cocktails and more live Hawaiian and pop-rock music poolside. (www.rumfirewaikiki.com; Sheraton Waikiki, 2255 Kalakaua Ave; ⊘noon-midnight)

Morimoto Waikiki, at Modern Honolulu

Addiction Nightclub & Lobby Bar
CLUB, BAR

Superstar mainland DJs and island dynamos spin at this boutique hotel's chic nightspot (see 27 ✕ Map p74, A1) with an upscale dress code (no shorts, flip-flops or hats). On special weekends, Addiction's daytime beach club lets you hang out on the pool deck with the sounds of electronica and techno grooves. (☎808-943-5800; www.addictionnightclub.com; Modern Honolulu, 1775 Ala Moana Blvd; ⊙nightclub 10:30pm-3am Thu-Sun, beach club noon-4pm Sat, lobby bar 6pm-late daily)

Five-0 Bar & Lounge
SPORTS BAR

You won't spot any *Hawaii Five-0* stars hiding out among the tropical la-

Local Life
People's Open Market
The city-sponsored **People's Open Market** (Map p75, G5; www.honolulu.gov/parks/dprpom.html; cnr Monsarrat & Paki Aves, Kapi'olani Park; ⊙10-11am Wed; 🚶) in Kapi'olani Park sees farmers trade in fresh bounty from *mauka* (the mountains) to *makai* (the sea). Only a short walk from Waikiki along Monsarrat Ave.

nai greenery inside this shopping-mall bar (see 36 ⭐ Map p74, D3), but it's still loads of fun with friends. Boogie down on the dance floor or twirl the swizzle stick in your mai tai while listening to live bands, then belly up to the

Understand
Eat Inland for Value

Along Kalakaua Ave, chains such as the Cheesecake Factory overflow with hungry tourists. A block inland, Kuhio Ave is great for cheap grazing, especially at multiethnic take-out joints.

On the outskirts of Waikiki, Kapahulu Ave is always worth a detour for its standout neighborhood eateries, drive-ins and bakeries, cooking up anything from Hawaiian soul food to Japanese country fare. Wander down past the zoo and Waikiki School to reach some great eating options up on Monsarrat Ave.

polished native-wood bar for *kalua* pork sliders. (📞808-922-0550; www.five-o-bar.com; 2nd fl, Bldg B, Royal Hawaiian Center, 2233 Kalakaua Ave; ⊙noon-midnight Mon-Thu, to 2am Fri & Sat, 11am-11pm Sun)

Lewers Lounge   LOUNGE

29 Map p74, C3

The nostalgic dream of Waikiki as an aristocratic playground is kept alive

Local Life
Waiola Shave Ice

Waiola Shave Ice (📞808-949-2269; waiolashaveice.com; 3113 Mokihana St; shave ice $2-5; ⊙11am-5:30pm Mon-Thu, to 6pm Fri-Sun; P🚻) still makes the same superfine shave ice as it did back in 1940, and we'd argue that it's got the formula exactly right. Get yours doused with 20-plus flavors of syrup and topped by azuki beans, *liliko'i* cream, condensed milk, Hershey's chocolate syrup or spicy-sweet *li hing mui* (crack seed).

at this Halekulani hotel bar. We're talking contemporary and classic cocktails, tempting appetizers and desserts, and smooth jazz combos that serenade after 8:30pm nightly. (2199 Kalia Rd, Halekulani; ⊙7:30pm-1am)

Genius Lounge   LOUNGE

Like a Japanese speakeasy, this glowing candle-lit hideaway (see 40 Map p74, D2) is a chill retreat for ultracool hipsters and lovebird couples. East-West tapas bites let you nibble on squid tempura, *loco moco* or banana cake while you sip made-in-Japan sake brews and retro jazz or cutting-edge electronica tickles your ears. (📞808-626-5362; www.geniusloungehawaii.com; 3rd fl, 346 Lewers St; ⊙6pm-2am)

Da Big Kahuna   BAR

30 Map p74, E2

Do you dream of a kitschy tiki bar where fruity, Kool Aid–colored drinks are poured into ceramic mugs carved

House Without a Key (p88)

with the faces of Polynesian gods? To get soused fast, order Da Fish Bowl – just don't try picking up a pool cue or shimmying on the small dance floor once you've drained it. Full food menu served till 3am. (☎808-923-0033; www. dabigkahuna.net; 2299 Kuhio Ave; ⏰10:30am-3am)

Nashville Waikiki
BAR, CLUB

31 Map p74, E2

Like Waikiki's own little honkytonk, this country-and-western dive bar can get as rowdy as a West Texas brawl. Homesick Southerners show up for sports TVs, billiards, darts, pool tournaments, and free line-dancing and two-steppin' lessons. Afternoon,

Local Life
Gay & Lesbian Waikiki

Waikiki's main gay venue, **Hula's Bar & Lei Stand** (Map p75, F4; ☎808-923-0669; www.hulas.com; 2nd fl, Castle Waikiki Grand, 134 Kapahulu Ave; ⏰10am-2am; 🛜), is a friendly, open-air bar. Hunker down at the pool table, or gaze at the spectacular vista of Diamond Head. The breezy balcony bar also has views of **Queen's Surf Beach**, a prime destination for a sun-worshipping LGBTQ crowd.

Top Tip

Sunset on the Beach

On some starry Saturday nights, Queen's Surf Beach turns into a festive scene. Dubbed **Sunset on the Beach** (Map p75; F5; www.sunsetonthebeach.net), tables and chairs are set up on the sand and live Hawaiian music acts perform on a beachside stage for about two hours before show time. When darkness falls, a huge screen is unscrolled and a feature movie is shown, starting around 7pm. Sometimes it's a film with island connections, such as *Blue Hawaii* (the 1961 classic starring Elvis Presley), while other nights it's a Hollywood blockbuster.

evening and late-night happy hours seem endless. (www.nashvillewaikiki.com; 2330 Kuhio Ave; ⏰4pm-4am)

Entertainment

House Without a Key

LIVE MUSIC, HULA

32 ⭐ Map p74, C3

Named after a 1925 Charlie Chan novel set in Honolulu, this genteel open-air hotel lounge sprawled beneath a century-old kiawe tree simply has no doors to lock. A sophisticated crowd gathers here for sunset cocktails, Hawaiian music and solo hula dancing by former Miss Hawaii pageant winners. Panoramic ocean views are as

intoxicating as the tropical cocktails. (📞808-923-2311; www.halekulani.com; Halekulani, 2199 Kalia Rd; ⏰7am-9pm)

Mai Tai Bar

LIVE MUSIC, HULA

At the Royal Hawaiian's low-key bar (see 11 ⊙ Map p74, D3) – no preppy resort wear required – you can catch some great acoustic island music acts and graceful solo hula dancers some nights. Even if you don't dig who's performing, the signature Royal Mai Tai still packs a punch and romantic views of the breaking surf extend down to Diamond Head. (📞808-923-7311; www.royal-hawaiian.com; Royal Hawaiian, 2259 Kalakaua Ave; ⏰10am-midnight)

Beach Bar

LIVE MUSIC, HULA

Inside this historic beachfront hotel bar (see 12 ⊙ Map p75, E3), soak up the sounds of classical and contemporary Hawaiian musicians playing underneath the old banyan tree where the *Hawaii Calls* radio program was broadcast nationwide during the mid-20th century. Live-music schedules vary, but hula soloists dance from 6pm to 8pm most nights. (📞808-922-3111; www.moana-surfrider.com; Moana Surfrider, 2365 Kalakaua Ave; ⏰10:30am-midnight)

Tapa Bar

LIVE MUSIC

33 ⭐ Map p74, B1

It's worth navigating through the gargantuan Hilton resort complex to this Polynesian-themed open-air bar just to see some of the best traditional and

Understand
Surfing

History of Hawaiian Surfing
The earliest written account of surfing is by Lieutenant James King, one of Captain Cook's men, in 1779. He devoted two full pages to a description of 'surfboard riding' in the voyage's journals. He could tell just how much fun the sport was, writing '...they seem to feel a great pleasure in the motion that this exercise gives.'

Surfing is believed to have originated long ago in ancient Polynesia, later thriving in Hawaii. By 1779, riding waves was an integral part of Hawaiian culture. With the arrival of western missionaries in the 1800s however, Hawaiian customs like *hula* and surfing were discouraged.

In the late 1800s King Kalakaua revived the *hula*, encouraging a return of Hawaiian cultural pride. In the early 1900s, surfing was revitalized on Waikiki Beach by Duke Kahanamoku and other beachboys, who taught visitors how to surf. Duke later became a gold-medal Olympic swimmer and known as the 'father of modern surfing,' spreading the sport to the mainland US and Australia.

Big Wave Surfing
In the 1950s surfers began to ride the powerful winter waves on O'ahu's North Shore and Leeward coasts. Big waves hit Hawaii between November and February and some of the world's best surfing competitions are held on O'ahu's North Shore in November and December, including the Vans Triple Crown of Surfing.

Surfing in Waikiki
Slow mellow combers (long, curling waves) provide the perfect training ground for beginners in Waikiki. Board rentals abound on central Waikiki Beach and local beachboys are always on hand for lessons at spots like mellow **Queens**, mushy **Canoes**, and gentle but crowded **Populars**. For surf reports, check out **Surf News Network** (www.surfnewsnetwork.com).

Surfing Tributes
In Waikiki, look out for the **statue of Duke Kahanamoku** on the waterfront on Kalakaua Ave. While critics say that Duke would never have his back to the sea, this much-loved statue of a real Hawaiian hero is often covered in flower lei. Further towards Diamond Head you'll find the **Surfer on a Wave statue**, celebrating surfing as a major part of the culture of Waikiki.

contemporary Hawaiian groups performing on Oʻahu today. There is live music nightly from 7.30pm or 8pm. (📞808-949-4321; www.hiltonhawaiianvillage.com; ground fl, Tapa Tower, Hilton Hawaiian Village, 2005 Kalia Rd; 🕙10am-11pm)

Moana Terrace   LIVE MUSIC

34 ⭐ Map p74, F4

If you're in a mellow mood, come for sunset happy-hour drinks at this casual, poolside bar, just a lei's throw from Kuhio Beach. Slack key guitarists, ukulele players and *haʻi* falsetto singers make merry for a family-friendly crowd. (📞808-922-6611; 2nd fl, Marriott Waikiki Beach Resort, 2552 Kalakaua Ave; 🕙11am-11pm;)

✅ Top Tip
What's On?

Whether you want to linger over one of those cool, frosty drinks with the little umbrellas or are craving live Hawaiian music and hula dancing, you're in the right place. For what's going on tonight, from DJ and live-music gigs to special events, check the **Honolulu Star-Advertiser's TGIF** (www.honolulu-pulse.com) section, which comes out every Friday, and the free alternative tabloid **Honolulu Weekly** (http://honoluluweekly.com/), published every Wednesday.

Kani Ka Pila Grille   LIVE MUSIC

35 ⭐ Map p74, C2

Once happy hour ends, the Outrigger's lobby bar sets the scene for some of the most laid-back live-music shows of any of Waikiki's beachfront hotels, with traditional and contemporary Hawaiian musicians playing their hearts out and cracking jokes. (📞808-924-4990; www.outriggerreef.com; Outrigger Reef on the Beach, 2169 Kalia Rd; 🕙11am-10pm)

Royal Grove   LIVE MUSIC, HULA

36 ⭐ Map p74, D3

This shopping mall's open-air stage may lack oceanfront views, but Hawaiian music and hula performances by top island talent happen here almost every evening, along with twice-weekly lunchtime shows by performers from the Windward Coast's Polynesian Cultural Center and concerts by the Royal Hawaiian Band. (📞808-922-2299; www.royalhawaiiancenter.com/info/entertainment; ground fl, Royal Hawaiian Center, 2201 Kalakaua Ave; admission free; 🕙schedules vary)

ʻAha ʻAina   LUAU

This oceanfront sit-down dinner show (see 11 Map p74, D3) is like a three-act musical play narrating the history of Hawaiian *mele* (songs) and hula. The food is top notch and there's an open bar. (📞808-921-4600; www.royal-hawaiian.com/dining/ahaaina; Royal Hawaiian, 2259 Kalakaua Ave; adult/child 5-12yr from $179/101; 🕙5:30-8pm Mon)

Royal Hawaiian Center

Waikiki Starlight Luau LUAU

37 ⭐ Map p74, B1

Enthusiastic pan-Polynesian show, with buffet meal, outdoor seating, Samoan fire dancing and *hapa haole* (literally, 'half foreign') hula. (☏808-947-2607; www.hiltonhawaiianvillage.com/luau; Hilton Hawaiian Village, 2005 Kalia Rd; adult/child 4-11yr from $99/50; ☺5:30-8pm Sun-Thu, weather permitting; 🖼)

Shopping

Royal Hawaiian Center MALL

Not to be confused with the Royal Hawaiian resort hotel next door, Waikiki's biggest shopping center (see 36 ⭐ Map p74, D3) has four levels and houses more than 80 breezily mixed stores. Look for Hawaii-born labels such as Noa Noa for Polynesian-print sarongs, sundresses and shirts. Art galleries display high-quality koa carvings, while jewelers trade in Ni'ihau shell-lei necklaces and flower lei stands sell fresh, wearable art. (www.royalhawaiiancenter.com; 2201 Kalakaua Ave; ☺10am-10pm)

Reyn Spooner CLOTHING

38 🔒 Map p74, D3

Since 1956, Reyn Spooner's subtly designed, reverse-print preppy aloha shirts have been the standard for Honolulu's businessmen, political power brokers and social movers-and-

Local Life

Feather Lei

At **Na Lima Mili Hulu No'eau** (Map p75, H2; ☎808-732-0865; 762 Kapahulu Ave; ⏰usually 9am-4pm Mon-Sat), the ancient craft of feather-lei making is alive and well. The store's name means 'the skilled hands that touch the feathers.' It can take days to produce a single feather lei, prized by collectors. Call ahead to check opening hours or make an appointment for a personalized lesson.

shakers. Reyn's Waikiki flagship is a bright, mod and clean-lined store, carrying colorful racks of men's shirts and board shorts, too. Also at Kahala Mall and Ala Moana Center. Ask about Reyn's Rack downtown for discounts on factory seconds. (☎808-923-7896; www.reynspooner.com; Sheraton Waikiki, 2259 Kalakaua Ave; ⏰8am-10:30pm)

Ukulele PuaPua   UKULELE

Avoid those flimsy souvenir ukuleles and head to one of PuaPua's two locations, one at the Sheraton Waikiki (see 12 ◉ Map p75, E3), the other nearby at the Moana Surfrider (see 12 ◉ Map p75, E3), to find the real thing. These guys are passionate and offer free group beginner lessons every day. (☎808-924-2266; www.hawaiianukuleleonline.com; Sheraton Waikiki, 2255 Kalakaua Ave; ⏰9am-10pm)

Newt at the Royal   CLOTHING

39 🔒 Map p74, D3

With stylish flair and panache, Newt specializes in Montecristi Panama hats – classic men's fedoras, plantation-style hats and women's *fino*. It also has fine reproductions of aloha shirts using 1940s and '50s designs. Everything's tropical, neat as a pin and top-drawer quality. (www.newtattheroyal.com; Royal Hawaiian, 2259 Kalakaua Ave; ⏰9am-9pm)

Genius Outfitters   ARTS, CRAFTS

40 🔒 Map p74, D2

This cutesy arts, crafts and clothing store on Lewers specializes in locally made goods. It covers the first two floors of an attractive three-story building with Genius Lounge on top. (☎808-922-2822; www.geniusoutfitters.net; 346 Lewers St; ⏰10.30am-10pm)

Peggy's Picks   COLLECTIBLES

41 🔒 Map p74, H2

Peggy's Picks on Kapahulu Ave is the place to go for Hawaiiana, treasures and collectibles from all over the world. It's a bit ramshackle and can get a tad crowded, but well worth it for the collectors among us. (☎808-737-3297; www.facebook.com/PeggysPicks; 732 Kapahalu Ave; ⏰11am-7pm Mon-Sat)

ROSAIRENEBETANCOURT 2 / ALAMY ©

Ukulele for sale

Island Paddler

CLOTHING

42 🔒 Map p74, H2

Besides having a great selection of paddles and paddling gear, these guys have T-shirts, aloha shirts, beach-wear and everything you might need for a day at the beach – along with a friendly and relaxed atmosphere. (📞 808-737-4854; www.islandpaddlerhawaii. com; 716 Kapahulu Ave; ⊙10am-6pm)

Art on the Zoo Fence

ARTS, CRAFTS

43 🔒 Map p74, F5

Dozens of artists hang their works along the fence on the south side of the Honolulu Zoo every weekend, weather permitting. Browse the contemporary watercolor, acrylic and oil paintings and colorful island photography as you chat with the artists themselves. (www.artonthezoofence. com; Monsarrat Ave, opposite Kapi'olani Park; ⊙9am-4pm Sat & Sun)

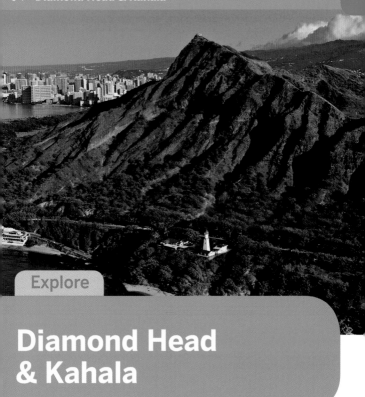

Explore

Diamond Head
& Kahala

Cue the *Hawaii Five-0* music and pretend to be a movie star as you cruise east from Waikiki through the glamorous suburb of Kahala, past the incomparable Diamond Head, O'ahu's best-known land-mark, and billionaire Doris Duke's former mansion, Shangri La. This affluent seaside suburb is home to many of O'ahu's wealthiest residents plus the island's most exclusive resort hotel.

The Sights in a Day

☀ You'll want to climb up **Diamond Head** (p96) earlyish to avoid the full heat of the day. If you've walked from Waikiki, refresh yourself at **Diamond Head Cove Health Bar** (p73) on Monsarrat Ave either on your way or on your way back. Alternatively, if it's a Saturday, drop in to the **KCC Farmers Market** (p102) at Kapiʻolani Community College.

☼ Take lunch at **Kahala Mall** (p103), before heading into town to the **Honolulu Museum of Art** (p46) – this is where all tours of Doris Duke's **Shangri La** (p98) leave from. It will be late afternoon by the time you're back in Kahala.

☽ Head to **Town** (p103) on Waiʻalae Ave for dinner, then depending on schedules, drop in to the **Movie Museum** (p103) close by, watch a movie back at **Kahala Mall** (p103), or best of all, watch a show at **Diamond Head Theatre** (p103).

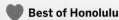 **Top Sights**

Diamond Head (p96)

Shangri La (p98)

💜 **Best of Honolulu**

Drinking & Entertainment
Diamond Head Theatre (p103)

Museums
Shangri La (p98)

For Kids
Kahala Mall (p103)

Outdoor Activities
Diamond Head (p96)

Getting There

🚌 **Bus** From Waikiki, catch TheBus 22, 23 or 24 for Diamond Head and Kahala Mall.

🚗 **Car** From Waikiki, head up Monsarrat Ave for Diamond Head. Hwy 1 ends at Kahala and becomes Kalanianaʻole Hwy out to Hawaiʻi Kai.

🚶 **Walking** Diamond Head is within walking distance of Waikiki.

Top Sights
Diamond Head

Is there a more recognizable backdrop in Hawaii? Named when British sailors thought they'd found diamonds here in 1825, this volcanic tuff cone and crater was used by ancient Hawaiians for human sacrifices. These days, even families with kids in tow can tackle the military-built 0.8-mile trail up to the windy summit with fantastic 360-degree views of the southeast coast to Koko Head and the Leeward Coast to the Wai'anae Range.

Map p100, B3

www.hawaiistateparks.org

off Diamond Head Rd btwn Makapu'u & 18th Aves

admission per pedestrian/car $1/5

6am-6pm, last trail entry 4:30pm

View from Diamond Head summit

Don't Miss

Tunnels and Stairs

Well you can't miss them if you're climbing to the summit, but take your time and enjoy them! The first set of 74 concrete steps is followed by a lighted 225ft-long tunnel. Next up is a set of 99 steep steps, then entry to the lowest level of the Fire Control Station.

Fire Control Station

The Fire Control Station was built to direct artillery fire from batteries at Fort DeRussy in Waikiki and Fort Ruger outside Diamond Head crater. Continue your adventure by climbing a lighted spiral staircase until you exit to the exterior of the crater. Finally, a set of 54 metal stairs that were installed in the 1970s to replace a ladder, takes you to the top. You're now at the crater summit and the uppermost level of the Fire Control Station (761ft). Enjoy the view!

The Loop Trail

Don't head back down the way you came. From the summit, follow the trail along the rim and descend the 82 metal steps down to the lower trail. The bunkers along the crater rim were built in 1915. Before heading down the Loop Trail, which will take you back to the top of the 225ft-long tunnel you went through earlier, wander out to the Lookout.

The Lookout

There are impressive views from the Lookout of the southeastern O'ahu coastline towards Koko Head. On a clear day you may even spot the islands of Moloka'i, Lana'i and Maui. If it's winter, keep an eye out for passing whales.

☑ Top Tips

▶ The state park has restrooms, drinking fountains, vending machines and a picnic area. There's plenty of parking; $5 entry for cars, cash only.

▶ The trail is mostly open and hot, so wear a hat and sunscreen and bring plenty of water. It's a good idea to get started early before the day heats up.

▶ Although fairly steep, the trail has tunnels and staircases, is partly paved and takes about an hour and a half round-trip.

✕ Take a Break

On your way back down to Waikiki, drop in at Diamond Head Cove Health Bar (p73), just up from Waikiki School, for one of their delicious acai bowls.

Top Sights
Shangri La

Doris Duke, the tobacco heiress who was once nicknamed 'the richest little girl in the world,' inherited an immense fortune in 1925 when her father died. Ten years later, on her honeymoon, she fell in love with O'ahu and subsequently built a dazzling oceanfront hideaway on Black Point, in the shadow of Diamond Head. Over the next 60 years she traveled the globe from Indonesia to Istanbul and stocked Shangri La with priceless Islamic art.

👁 Map p100, C4

📞 808-532-3853

www.shangrilahawaii.org

2½hr tour incl transportation $25

🕐 tours 9am, 10:30am & 1:30pm Wed-Sat, closed early Sep–early Oct

Pool and the Playhouse, Shangri La

Don't Miss

The Mughal Suite

Newly renovated and first opened to the public in 2014, this bedroom and bathroom suite is a set of rooms that Doris Duke (1912–93) commissioned architect Frances Blomfield in Delhi, India to design while on her 1935 honeymoon. The suite, originally designed to be for Duke's personal use, reflects the rooms' earliest completed appearance in 1939 as shown in photographs in the architect's album.

The Damascus Room

In 1952, Doris Duke purchased 'one old Damascus Room made of old painted panels of wood.' The room, which would have originally decorated a reception room of an affluent courtyard home in Syria, is now a highlight of the Islamic art collection and was first opened to the public in 2012.

The Mughal Garden

The idea for Shangri La's Mughal Garden was based on royal gardens found throughout the Indian subcontinent. During her 1935 honeymoon travels in India, Doris Duke was exposed to the sumptuous gardens of the high Mughal period, particularly those built in the cities of Agra, Delhi and Lahore.

Playhouse

At the western end of Shangri La and adjacent to the ocean, the Playhouse is a poolside pavilion inspired by the Chehel Sutun palace in Isfahan, the capital of Iran from 1598 to 1722. Featuring a large living room, a kitchen and two bedroom suites, it has a large deck with a painted wood ceiling supported by 14 columns, facing a gorgeous pool.

☑ Top Tips

▶ Shangri La can only be visited on a guided tour departing from downtown's Honolulu Museum of Arts, where you'll watch a brief background video first, then travel as a group by minibus to the estate.

▶ Tours often sell out weeks ahead of time, so make reservations as far ahead as possible at www.honolulumuseum. org.

▶ Shangri La is closed to tours from early September to early October.

✖ Take a Break

A brilliant option either before or after your tour, the Honolulu Museum of Arts Cafe (p54) is open for lunch from Tuesday to Saturday.

Waialae
Country Club

Waialae
Beach Park

Maunalua
Bay

KAHALA

Kealaolu Ave

Kahala Ave

Lunalilo Fwy

Hunakai St

Hunakai St

Black Point
(Kupikipiki'o)

Pacific Ocean

Diamond Head
Memorial Park
(Cemetery)

Shangri La

Monsarrat Ave

Wilhelmina St

Wai'alae Ave

KAIMUKI

Kilauea Ave

12th Ave

Kuilei Cliffs
Beach Park

Harding Ave

Lunalilo Fwy

Diamond
Head

Diamond Head Rd

Alohea Ave

Monsarrat Ave

Diamond Head
Beach Park

Lincoln Ave

Kaimuki Ave

Olu St

Date St

Mooheau
Ave

Castle St

Winam Ave

Campbell Ave

Kanaina Ave

Monsarrat Ave

Kanaina Ave

Ala Wai
Golf Course

Kapahulu Ave

Honolulu
Zoo

Leahi Ave
Paki Ave

Leahi Ave

Paki Ave

Kapi'olani
Park

Kapi'olani
Beach Park

Kalakaua Ave

Sans Souci
Beach Park

Ala Wai Canal

Ala Wai Blvd

1 km
0.5 miles

Wai'alae Beach Park

Sights

Diamond Head Beach Park
BEACH

1 Map p100, B4

Bordering the lighthouse, this rocky beach occasionally draws surfers, snorkelers and tide-poolers, plus a few picnickers. The narrow strand nicknamed Lighthouse Beach is popular with gay men, who head off Diamond Head Rd onto short, dead-end Beach Rd, then walk east along the shore to find a little seclusion and (illegally) sunbathe au naturel. (3300 Diamond Head Rd)

Kuilei Cliffs Beach Park
BEACH

2 Map p100, B4

In the shadow of Diamond Head, this rocky beach draws experienced windsurfers when the tradewinds are blowing. When the swells are up, surfers take over the waves. The little beach has outdoor showers but no other facilities. You'll find paved parking lots off Diamond Head Rd, just east of the lighthouse. (3450 Diamond Head Rd)

Wai'alae Beach Park
BEACH

3 Map p100, E2

At this picturesque sandy beach, a gentle stream meets the sea. Local surfers challenge Razors, a break off the channel's west side. Swimming conditions are usually calm, though not the best due to the shallow reef. A favorite of wedding parties, the beach park has shady picnic tables, restrooms and outdoor showers. The parking lot is often full. (4925 Kahala Ave)

O'ahu's Top Farmers Market

At O'ahu's premier gathering of farmers and their fans, the **KCC Farmers Market** (Map p100, C2; http://hfbf.org/markets; parking lot C, Kapi'olani Community College, 4303 Diamond Head Rd; ⏰7:30-11am Sat; 🅿️🚻), everything sold is locally made or grown and has a loyal following, from Nalo greens to Kahuku shrimp and corn. Get there early for the best of everything.

Eating

Hoku's

PACIFIC RIM **$$$**

 4 Map p100, E2

Chef Wayne Hirabayashi is revered for his elegant East-West creations such as braised short ribs with avocado tempura and wok-fried market-fresh fish paired with a world-ranging wine list. Sunday brunch buffet stars a seafood raw bar piled high with all-you-can-eat king-crab legs and a chocolate dessert fountain. Make reservations and inquire about the dress code. (📞808-739-8760; www.kahalaresort.com; Kahala Hotel & Resort, 5000 Kahala Ave; Sun brunch adult/child 6-12yr $65/33, dinner mains $30-65; ⏰10am-2pm Sun, 5:30-10pm Wed-Sun)

Whole Foods

SUPERMARKET **$**

Fill your picnic basket here (see 10 ⭐ Map p100, D2) with organic produce and locally made specialty foods, hot and cold deli items, takeout sushi and salads, made-to-order hot pizzas and imported wines. (http://wholefoods market.com; Kahala Mall, 4211 Wai'alae Ave; ⏰7am-10pm; 🅿️)

Crack Seed Store

SWEETS **$**

 5 Map p100, C1

Mom-and-pop candy store on a side street in Kaimuki vends overflowing glass jars of made-from-scratch crack seed, plus addictive frozen slushies spiked with *li hing mui* (salty dried plums). (📞818-737-1022; 1156 Koko Head Ave; ⏰9.30am-6pm Mon-Sat, midday-4pm Sun; 🚻)

12th Avenue Grill

MODERN AMERICAN **$$**

6 Map p100, C1

Hidden in a side road off Wai'alae Ave, this Kaimuki grill has been picking up a number of best restaurant awards of late. Combining the efforts of an impressive team and using as much local produce as possible, 12th Ave Grill has the locals drooling. (📞808-732-9469; http://12thavegrill.com; 1120 12th Ave; mains $18-36; ⏰5:30-10pm Sun-Thu, to 11pm Fri & Sat)

Salt Kitchen & Tasting Bar

MODERN AMERICAN **$$**

 7 Map p100, C1

Mexican oxtail empanadas, Italian ravioli made with Hawaii-grown squash, and Indian naan with pickled eggplant fill the tapas-sized plates lined up all along the lacquered bar top. Bartenders shake up grapefruit daiquiris and tequila martinis for a chic crowd of urbane revelers during afternoon happy hours in the Kaimuki neighborhood.

(☎808-744-7567; http://salthonolulu.com; 3605
Wai'alae Ave; shared plates $5-21, mains $10-25;
⏰5pm-midnight Sun-Thu, to 1am Fri & Sat)

Town
FUSION $$

8 🍴 Map p100, B1

At this hip modern coffee shop and
bistro hybrid in Kaimuki, the motto is
'local first, organic whenever possible,
with aloha always.' On the daily-chang-
ing menu of boldly flavored cooking
are burgers and steaks made from
North Shore free-range cattle and sal-
ads that taste as if the ingredients were
just plucked from a backyard garden.
(☎808-735-5900; www.townkaimuki.com;
3435 Wai'alae Ave; mains breakfast & lunch $5-
16, dinner $16-26; ⏰7am-2:30pm daily, plus
5:30-9:30pm Mon-Thu, to 10pm Fri & Sat)

Entertainment

Diamond Head Theatre
THEATER

9 ⭐ Map p100, B2

Opened in 1915 and known as 'the
Broadway of the Pacific,' this lovely
old theater is the third oldest continu-
ously running community theater in
the USA. Runs a variety of high-
quality shows throughout the year
with everything from Mary Poppins to
Spamalot to South Pacific. Also runs
acting, dancing and singing classes.
(☎808-733-0277; www.diamondheadtheatre.
com; 520 Makapuu Ave)

Kahala Mall
CINEMA

10 ⭐ Map p100, D2

Eight-screen multiplex frequently
screens independent arthouse and for-

Local Life

Tamura's Poke

Arguably the best *poke* on the island
is in undistinguished-looking **Ta-
mura's** (☎808-735-7100; www.tamu-
rasfinewine.com/pokepage.html; 3496
Wai'alae Ave, Kaimuki; ⏰11am-8.45pm
Mon-Fri, 9.30am-8.45pm Sat, 9.30am-
7:45pm Sun; P). The sign says Fine
Wines & Liquors, but head inside,
turn right and wander down to
poke corner. The 'spicy ahi' and the
smoked marlin is to die for. Ask for
tasters before buying take away.

eign films. (☎movie infoline 808-593-3000;
www.kahalamallcenter.com; 4211 Wai'alae Ave)

Movie Museum
CINEMA

11 ⭐ Map p100, C1

In the Kaimuki neighborhood, east of
the UH Manoa campus, this sociable
spot screens classic, foreign and indie
films, including some Hawaii premieres,
in a tiny theater equipped with digital
sound and just 20 comfy Barca-loungers.
Reservations recommended. (☎808-735-
8771; www.kaimukihawaii.com; 3566 Harding
Ave; tickets $5; ⏰noon-9pm Thu-Mon)

Shopping

Kahala Mall
MALL

It's no competition for the Ala Moana
Center, but this neighborhood mall (see
10 ⭐ Map p100, D2) has a noteworthy mix
of only-in-Hawaii shops; look for aloha
shirts and collectible, hard-to-find
imported Hello Kitty toys and logo gear.
(www.kahalamallcenter.com; 4211 Wai'alae Ave;
⏰10am-9pm Mon-Sat, to 6pm Sun)

Explore

Hawai'i Kai & Southeast O'ahu

Towards the eastern end of O'ahu, the Kalaniana'ole Hwy (Hwy 72) becomes a slow-and-go coastal drive that swells and dips like the sea itself as it rounds ancient volcanic Koko Head. The snorkeling hot-spot of Hanauma Bay, hiking trails on Kuli'ou'ou Ridge and windy Makapu'u Point, and O'ahu's most famous body-boarding beaches are all just a short ride from Waikiki.

The Sights in a Day

Get to **Hanauma Bay** (p106) nice and early to avoid the crowds and the heat. When you've had enough of snorkeling, drive the sights of O'ahu's southeast coast, stopping at **Lana'i Lookout** (p109), **Halona Blowhole** (p109), **Sandy Beach Park** (p109) and **Makapu'u Beach Park** (p110). If it's a clear day, take a walk up the **Makapu'u Point Lighthouse Trail** (p110) to check out the views.

Back in Hawai'i Kai, some sustenance must be in order. For a local-style plate-lunch, head into **Fatboy's** (p111), or for something lighter, try **Kokonuts Shave Ice & Snacks** (p111), both at Koko Marina. Try out some of the watersports on offer at the marina, or take a walk at **Koko Crater Botanical Garden** (p109).

Once it's time for an Hawaii brew, head to **Kona Brewing Company** (p111) at Koko Marina for dinner and drinks.

 Top Sights

Hanauma Bay (p106)

 Best of Honolulu

Beaches
Hanauma Bay (p106)

Sandy Beach Park (p109)

Eating
Bubbies (p111)

Drinking & Entertainment
Kona Brewing Company (p111)

Hikes
Kuli'ou'ou Ridge Trail (p110)

Koko Crater Trail (p110)

Makapu'u Point Lighthouse Trail (p110)

Gardens, Sanctuaries & Cemeteries
Koko Crater Botanical Garden (p109)

Getting There

🚌 **Bus** From Waikiki, TheBus 22 stops at Koko Marina Center (30 minutes) en route to Hanauma Bay; TheBus 23 turns inland at Keahole St.

🚗 **Car** It takes about 20 minutes to drive to Hawai'i Kai from Waikiki. Take H-1 which turns into the Kanaliana'ole Hwy – and carries on around Makapu'u Point to the Windward Coast.

Top Sights
Hanauma Bay

An absolute gem, Hanauma Bay is one of the world's top spots to get an up-close look at spectacular sea life. Protected by a 7000-year old coral reef that stretches across the width of the bay, snorkelers can paddle about and come face-to-face with an amazingly colorful array of tropical fish. You're bound to see schools of glittering silver fish, the bright-blue flash of parrotfish, and perhaps sea turtles so used to snorkelers they're ready to go eyeball-to-mask with you.

Map p108, C4

808-396-4229

www.honolulu.gov/parks/facility/hanaumabay

adult/child under 13yr $7.50/free

6am-6pm Wed-Mon Nov-Mar, to 7pm Wed-Mon Apr-Oct

Sunrise over Hanauma Bay

Don't Miss

For First-Timers

The bay is well protected from the ocean by reefs and the inlet's natural curve, making conditions favorable for snorkeling year-round. The fringing reef closest to shore has a large, sandy opening known as the Keyhole Lagoon, which is the best place for novice snorkelers. The deepest water is 10ft, though it's very shallow over the coral. Be careful not to step on the coral or to accidentally knock it with your fins.

For Confident Snorkelers

For confident snorkelers and strong swimmers, it's better on the outside of the reef, where there are large coral heads, bigger fish and fewer people; to get there follow the directions on the signboards or ask the lifeguard at the southern end of the beach. Don't attempt to swim outside the reef when the water is rough. Not only are the channel currents too strong, but the sand will be stirred up and visibility poor.

For Scuba-Divers

If you're scuba diving, you'll have the whole bay to play in, with crystal-clear water, coral gardens and sea turtles. Beware of currents when the surf's up, especially those surges near the shark-infested Witches Brew, on the bay's right-hand side, and the amusingly named Moloka'i Express, a treacherous current on the left-hand side of the bay's mouth.

☑ Top Tips

▶ To beat the crowds, arrive as soon as the park opens.

▶ All built park facilities are wheelchair accessible. Beach wheelchairs for visitors with mobility issues are available free of charge from the information kiosk between 8am and 4pm on a first-come, first-served basis.

▶ Feeding the fish is strictly prohibited, to preserve the delicate ecological balance of the bay. Despite its protected status, this beloved bay is still a threatened ecosystem, always in danger of being loved to death.

✗ Take a Break

On your way back to Honolulu or Waikiki, drop into the Koko Marina Center for a refreshing *mochi* ice cream at Bubbies (p111) or a visit to Kokonuts Shave Ice & Snacks (p111).

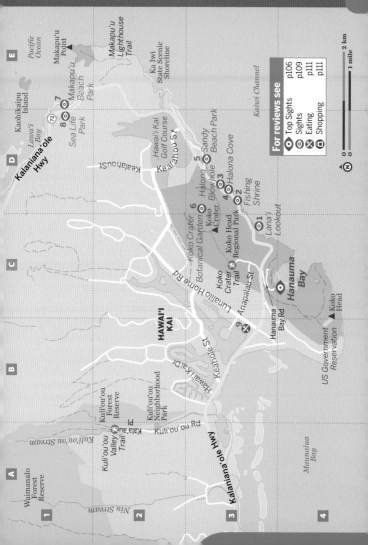

Pacific Ocean

Makapu'u Point

Makapu'u Lighthouse Trail

Ka Iwi State Scenic Shoreline

Makapu'u Beach Park

Kaohikaipu Island

Lana'i Lookout

Kealahou St

Hawai'i Kai Golf Course

Sandy Beach Park

Hālona Blowhole

Hālona Cove

Fishing Shrine

Koko Crater Botanical Garden

Koko Crater

Koko Head Regional Park

Koko Crater Trail

Hanauma Bay

Koko Head

US Government Reservation

Lunalilo Home Rd

Anapalau St

Hanauma Bay Rd

Keahole St

HAWAI'I KAI

Hawai'i Kai Dr

Kuli'ou'ou Forest Reserve

Kuli'ou'ou Neighborhood Park

Kaiau'u Pl

Kuli'ou'ou Rd

Kuli'ou'ou Valley Trail

Kalaniana'ole Hwy

Waimanalo Forest Reserve

Kuli'ou'ou Stream

Niu Stream

Maunalua Bay

Kaiwi Channel

Kalaniana'ole Hwy

Lawa'i Bay

Sea Life Park

For reviews see

◆ Top Sights   p106
◉ Sights   p109
✕ Eating   p111
🛍 Shopping   p111

2 km
1 mile

Sights

Lana'i Lookout
LOOKOUT

1 ◉ Map p108, C3

Less than a mile east of Hanauma Bay, roadside Lana'i Lookout offers a panorama on clear days of several Hawaiian islands: Lana'i to the right, Maui in the middle and Moloka'i to the left. It's also a good vantage point for getting a look at lava-rock formations that form the sea cliffs along this coast.

Fishing Shrine
SHRINE

2 ◉ Map p108, D3

As you drive east, make sure to keep your eyes toward the ocean. At the highest point, you should spot a templelike mound of rocks. The rocks surround a statue of Jizō, who is a Japanese Buddhist deity and a guardian of fishers. The fishing shrine is often decked out in flower lei and surrounded by sake cups. There is a little roadside pull-off in front of the shrine, about half-mile east of the Lana'i Lookout. (Kalaniana'ole Hwy)

Halona Blowhole
LOOKOUT

3 ◉ Map p108, D3

Just watch where all the tour buses are turning off to find this one. Here, ocean waves surge through a submerged tunnel in the rock and spout up through a hole in the ledge. It's preceded by a gushing sound, created by the air that's being forced out of the tunnel by rushing water. The action depends on water conditions – sometimes it's barely discernible, while at other times it's a real showstopper.

Halona Cove
BEACH

4 ◉ Map p108, D3

Take your lover down for a roll in the sand at this sweet pocket cove made famous in the steamy love scene between Burt Lancaster and Deborah Kerr in the 1953 movie *From Here to Eternity*. You can peer down at the cove from the Halona Blowhole parking lot, from where you'll just be able to make out a path leading down to the beach.

Sandy Beach Park
BEACH

5 ◉ Map p108, D3

Here the ocean heaves and thrashes like a furious beast. This is one of O'ahu's most dangerous beaches, with a punishing shorebreak, powerful backwash and strong rip currents. Expert bodysurfers and bodyboarders spend hours trying to mount the skull-crushing waves, as crowds gather to watch the daredevils being tossed around. Sandy Beach is wide, very long and, yes, sandy, but this is no place to frolic for the inexperienced – dozens of people are injured every year. (8800 Kalaniana'ole Hwy)

Koko Crater Botanical Garden
GARDENS

6 ◉ Map p108, D3

According to Hawaiian legend, Koko Crater is the imprint left by the

---

Understand
Watersports & Walking

Hawai'i Kai marina is flush with tour operators and watersports outfitters that can hook you up with jet packs, jet skis, banana and bumper boats, parasailing trips, wakeboarding, scuba dives, speed sailing – whatever will get your adrenaline pumping, they can hook you up, but it'll cost you plenty.

If you're after something more sedate, there are some excellent walks in the area. The **Kuli'ou'ou Ridge Trail** (https://hawaiitrails.ehawaii.gov) heads up a rough track into the mountains to the north of the Hawai'i Kai marina; the **Koko Crater Trail** climbs straight up the side of volcanic Koko Crater; and the **Makapu'u Point Lighthouse Trail** (www.hawaiistateparks.org; off Makapu'u Lighthouse Rd; ⏰7am-7:45pm Apr-1st Mon in Sep, 7am-6:45pm 1st Tue in Sep-Mar) runs up a mile-long paved road to the red-roofed Makapu'u Lighthouse.

---

magical flying vagina of Kapo, sent from the Big Island to lure the pig-god Kamapua'a away from Kapo's sister Pele, the Hawaiian goddess of fire and volcanoes. Inside the crater today is a quiet, county-run botanical garden abloom with flowering aloe plants and *wiliwili* trees, fragrant plumeria, spiny cacti and other native and exotic dryland species. Connecting loop trails lead through the lonely garden. (www.honolulu.gov/parks/hbg.html; end of Kokonani St; ⏰9am-4pm, closed Dec 25 & Jan 1)

Makapu'u Beach Park   BEACH
7   Map p108, E1

Opposite Sea Life Park, Makapu'u Beach is one of O'ahu's top winter bodyboarding and bodysurfing spots, with waves reaching 12ft and higher. It also has the island's best shorebreak. As with Sandy Beach Park, Makapu'u

is strictly the domain of experts who can handle rough water and dangerous currents. In summer, when the wave action disappears, calmer waters allow swimming. The beach park has restrooms, outdoor showers, drinking water and lifeguards. (41-095 Kalaniana'ole Hwy)

Sea Life Park   THEME PARK
8   Map p108, D1

Hawaii's only marine-life park offers a small mixed bag of rundown attractions. The theme-park entertainment features animals that aren't found in Hawaiian waters, though it also maintains a breeding colony of green sea turtles, releasing young hatchlings back into the wild every year. (☎808-259-2500; www.sealifeparkhawaii.com; 41-202 Kalaniana'ole Hwy; adult/child 3-11yr $30/20; ⏰10:30am-5pm; 🚼)

Eating

Bubbles
ICE CREAM $

9 Map p108, B3

Could it possibly get any better than a Bubbies *mochi* ice cream? We don't think so! There are so many great flavors to try that it will be hard to stop, especially after a day at the beach. (☎808-396-8722; www.bubbiesicecream.com; Koko Marina Center, 7192 Kalaniana'ole Hwy; items $1.50-6; ☺10am-11pm; 🖼)

Fatboy's
HAWAIIAN $

Slightly indelicately named, Fatboy's (see 9 🍴 Map p108, B3) handle says it all. If you're into Hawaiian-style plate lunches, then Fatboy's at Koko Marina ticks all the boxes. The Garlic Chicken ($8.99) gets rave reviews, but it's the Fatboy's Bento ($7.99) that has sold over 500,000 plates through the Fatboy's O'ahu stores. The full tables are testament to Fatboy's popularity. (☎808-394-2373; http://fatboyshawaii.com; Koko Marina Center, 7192 Kalaniana'ole Hwy; ☺8am-8pm)

Kona Brewing Company
PUB $$

On the docks of Koko Marina, this Big Island import (see 9 🍴 Map p108, B3) is known for its microbrewed beers, especially the Longboard Lager, the Pipeline Porter and the Big Wave Golden Ale. There's live Hawaiian music some nights, and the brewpub's island-style *pupu* (appetizers), wood-fired pizzas, burgers, seafood and

Top Tip

Kokonuts at Koko Marina
After a tough day at Hanauma Bay, do as President Obama has done (attested to by photos of Obama in a Kokonuts Shave Ice T-shirt!) and drop into **Kokonuts Shave Ice & Snacks** (Map p108, B3; ☎808-396-8809; Koko Marina Center, 7192 Kalaniana'ole Hwy; ☺10.30am-9pm) at Koko Marina. The acai and pitaya bowls are top notch, the shave ice really hits the spot, and the welcome is friendly. Good aloha here!

salads are filling. But it's the beer that makes this place! (☎808-396-5662; www.konabrewingco.com; Koko Marina Center, 7192 Kalaniana'ole Hwy; mains $12-28; ☺11am-10pm; 🖼)

Shopping

Island Treasures at the Marina
ARTS, CRAFTS

Near the waterfront at Koko Marina, this locally owned shop (see 9 🍴 Map p108, B3) displays high-quality artisan handiwork such as koa wood carvings, etched glass, pottery and island paintings. Handmade soaps, lotions and jewelry make memorable gifts. (☎808-396-8827; Koko Marina Center, 7192 Kalaniana'ole Hwy; ☺10am-6pm Mon-Sat, 11am-4pm Sun)

Explore

Kailua & Kane'ohe

On O'ahu's lushest, most verdant coast, *pali* (cliffs) are shrouded in mist as often as they are bathed in glorious sunshine. Tropical showers guarantee that everything glistens with a hundred shades of green, all dazzlingly set against turquoise bays and white-sand beaches. Repeat visitors to O'ahu often make this quiet side of the island their adventure base camp.

The Sights in a Day

 Start your morning with breakfast at **Morning Brew Coffee House & Bistro** (p122) in Kailua before heading down for some sand time at **Kailua Beach Park** (p116). Plenty of options for exercise here. Wander around to **Kalapawai Market** (p122) when you feel the need for refreshments.

 Take to the road for the afternoon. Visit Kailua's ancient temple at **Ulupo Heiau State Monument** (p117) before heading northwest to Kane'ohe. Drop in to see the 'fish art' at **Gyotaku by Naoki** (p118), then visit **Valley of the Temples & Byōdō-in** (p117) and **Ho'omaluhia Botanical Garden** (p118).

 Drive down to Waimanalo, check out the **Akebono Statue** (p119), then take a stroll at **Waimanalo Bay Beach Park** (p116) to start the evening. When it's time for dinner, head down the road to **Serg's Mexican Kitchen Nalo** (p120). For a post-dinner drink, head back into town to **Kailua Town Pub & Grill** (p122).

 Best of Honolulu

Beaches
Waimanalo Bay Beach Park (p116)

Bellows Field Beach Park (p116)

Kailua Beach Park (p116)

Lanikai Beach (p116)

Hawaiiana Shopping
Naturally Hawaiian Gallery (p123)

Gyotaku by Naoki (p118)

Gardens, Sanctuaries & Cemeteries
Ho'omaluhia Botanical Garden (p118)

Kawai Nui Marsh (p118)

Hamakua Marsh Wildlife Sanctuary (p118)

Valley of the Temples & Byōdō-In (p117)

Getting There

🚌 **Bus** TheBus 57 runs over the Pali Hwy to Kailua, then south to Waimanalo and Sea Life Park. TheBus 22 and 23 run around the eastern coast to Sea Life Park.

🚗 **Car** Drive the coast east along the Kanaliana'ole Hwy, round the eastern tip of the island; then drive back across the Pali Hwy to Honolulu.

A

'AHUIMANU

Kahalu'u Stream

Kahekili Hwy

Valley of the Temples

83

Valley of the Temples & Byōdō-In **7**

Pu'u Kawipo'o (2441ft)

He'eia Stream

Waiahole Forest Reserve

B

He'eia Pier **9**

He'eia State Park

He'eia Fishpond

HE'EIA

Haiku Rd

Lilipuna Rd

Kahuhipa St

Kāne'ohe District Park

Kāne'ohe Stream

C

Kealohi Point

Moku o Lo'e (Coconut Island)

Kane'ohe Bay

830

D

1

2

Moanalua Stream

H3

Omega Coast Guard Station

Kane'ohe Forest Reserve

Likelike Hwy

KĀNE'OHE

630

Kane'ohe Bay Dr

Mokapu Saddle Rd

Quarry Rd

3

Honolulu Watershed Forest Reserve

63

8

Ho'omaluhia Botanical Garden

83

Kamehameha Hwy

Hawaiian Memorial Park Cemetery

H3

Kalaniana'ole Hwy

Ko'olau Golf Club

Pali Golf Course

61

4

Likelike Hwy

63

Kamanaiki Stream

Honolulu Watershed Forest Reserve

61

Nu'uanu Reservoir

Pali Hwy

Nu'uanu Stream

Nu'uanu Pali State Wayside

Konahuanui (3105ft)

Maunawili Trail

Pali Hwy

MAUNAWILI

Omao Stream

5

PU'UNUI

61

Ninole Stream

Judd Trail

Pauoa (1194ft)

Nu'uanu Trail

Pauoa Flats

'Aihualama Trail

Lua'alaea Stream

Mt Olympus (2486ft)

P

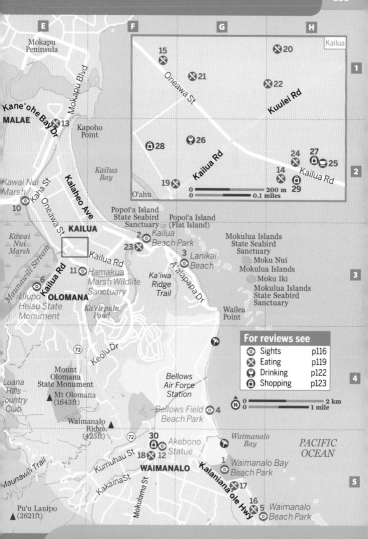

E

Mokapu
Peninsula

Kane'ohe Bay Dr
MALAE ⊗13

Kapoho
Point

Kailua
Bay

Kawai Nui ⊙ 10
Marsh

Kawai
Nui
Marsh

KAILUA

Kailua Rd

⊙ 6 ⊙ 11 ⊙ Hamakua
OLOMANA Marsh Wildlife
Sanctuary
Ulupō
Heiau State
Monument
Ka'elepulu
Pond

Luana
Hills
Country
Club

Mount
Olomana
State Monument
▲ Mt Olomana
(1643ft)

Waimanalo
Ridge
(425ft) ▲

Maunawili Trail

Pu'u Lanipo
(2621ft)

Keolu Dr

72

Kumuhau St
18⊙⊙12

Kakaina St
WAIMANALO

Mokulama St

F

15 ⊗

Oneawa St

⊗21

🅿26

28 19 ⊗

O'ahu

Popoi'a Island
State Seabird
Sanctuary
⊙ 2 ⊙ Kailua
23 ⊙ Beach Park

⊙ 3 ⊙ Lanikai
A'alapapa Dr Beach

Ka'iwa
Ridge
Trail

G

⊗20

⊗22

Kuulei Rd

Kailua Rd

14 24 27
⊗ 🅿25
29

Kailua Rd

0   200 m
0   0.1 miles

Popoi'a Island
(Flat Island)

Mokulua Islands
State Seabird
Sanctuary
Moku Nui
Mokulua Islands
Moku Iki
Mokulua Islands
State Seabird
Sanctuary
Wailea
Point

Bellows
Air Force
Station
⊙ Bellows Field 4
Beach Park

30
⊙⊙
Akebono
Statue

Waimanalo
Bay

⊙ 1
Waimanalo Bay
Beach Park

Kalaniana'ole Hwy

⊗17

16 ⊙ 5 Waimanalo
Beach Park

H

Kailua

1

2

3

For reviews see
⊙	Sights	p116
⊗	Eating	p119
🅿	Drinking	p122
🔒	Shopping	p123

Ⓝ 0   2 km
0   1 mile

PACIFIC
OCEAN

4

5

Sights

Waimanalo Bay
Beach Park BEACH

1 ⊚ Map p114, G5

A wide forest of ironwoods hides a broad sandy beach with little development in sight. This 75-acre county park has Waimanalo Bay's biggest waves and is popular with board surfers and bodyboarders. Even if you're not planning to hit the water, just take a walk along the cream-colored sand and try to imagine the feeling of old Hawaii. Countless weddings take place on this enchanting beach. There are lifeguards, campsites and restrooms. Entrance is opposite the Honolulu Polo Club. (Kalaniana'ole Hwy/Hwy 72)

Kailua Beach Park BEACH

2 ⊚ Map p114, F3

A wide arc of sand drapes around the jewel-colored waters of Kailua Bay, with formidable volcanic headlands bookending either side and interesting little islands rising off shore. It's ideal for long, leisurely walks, family outings and all kinds of aquatic activities. The beach has a gently sloping sandy bottom with usually calm waters; it's good for swimming year-round, especially in the morning.

Lanikai Beach BEACH

3 ⊚ Map p114, G3

Just southeast of Kailua, Lanikai is an exclusive residential neighborhood

fronting a gorgeous stretch of powdery white sand overlooking two postcard-perfect islands, known locally as the Mokes. Today the beach is shrinking: nearly half the sand has washed away as a result of retaining walls built to protect the neighborhood's multimillion-dollar mansions. There are 11 narrow public beach-access walkways off Mokulua Dr. No bathrooms, no lifeguards. (off Mokolua Dr)

Bellows Field Beach Park BEACH

4 ⊚ Map p114, G4

With fine sand and a natural setting backed by ironwood trees in places, this is a great beach. The only problem is that the park is only open to civilians on weekends (and national holidays) because it fronts Bellows Air Force Station. The small shorebreak waves are good for beginning bodyboarders and board surfers. Lifeguards, showers, restrooms, drinking water and camping are all available onsite. The park entrance is just north of Waimanalo Bay Beach Park. (Tinker Rd, off Kalaniana'ole Hwy/Hwy 72); ⊙open to public noon Fri-8am Mon, gates closed 8pm-6am)

Waimanalo Beach Park BEACH

5 ⊚ Map p114, G5

By the side of the roadway south of the main business area, this sloping strip of soft white sand has little puppy waves that are excellent for swimming. Manana Island and Makapu'u Point are visible to the south. The facilities include a huge grassy picnic

ANNA GORIN / GETTY IMAGES ©

Byōdō-in

area, restrooms, ball-sports courts, a playground and a rather unappealing campground. Lifeguards are on watch here. (Kalaniana'ole Hwy/Hwy 72)

Ulupo Heiau State Monument

TEMPLE

6   Map p114, E3

Rich in stream-fed agricultural land, abundant fishing grounds and protected canoe landings, Kailua was an ancient economic center that supported at least three temples. Ulupo, once bordered by 400 acres of cultivated fishponds and taro fields, is the only one left to visit. (www.hawaiistateparks. org; admission free; ☉sunrise-sunset)

Valley of the Temples & Byōdō-in

TEMPLE

7   Map p114, B1

So peaceful and park-like, it might take you a minute to realize Valley of the Temples is an interdenominational cemetery. Up at the base of the Ko'olau mountain's verdant fluted cliffs sits Byōdō-in, a replica of a 900-year-old temple in Uji, Japan. The symmetry is a classic example of Japanese Heian architecture, with rich vermilion walls. The 3-ton brass bell is said to bring peace and good fortune to anyone who rings it. (www.byodo-in.com; 47-200 Kahekili Hwy; temple admission adult/child under 13yr/ senior $3/1/2; ☉9am-5pm)

Gyotaku Fish Prints

You'll probably have seen Naoki's magnificent *gyotaku* (Japanese-style fish prints) all over O'ahu in galleries, restaurants and bars, but there's nothing like watching him print up a freshly caught fish in his own studio, **Gyotaku by Naoki** (Map p114, C2; ☑1-866-496-8258; http://gyotaku.com; 46-020 Alaloa St, Unit D, Kane'ohe), in Kane'ohe. All the fish he prints are eaten later and the spectacular art on hand is for sale. Call ahead to check the studio is open because Naoki is often out fishing.

Ho'omaluhia Botanical Garden

GARDENS

8 ◎ Map p114, C3

Beneath the dramatic ridged cliffs of the Ko'olau Range, O'ahu's largest botanical garden encompasses 400 acres of trees and shrubs from around the world. Plants are arranged in six regionally themed areas accessible by car. Pick up a map at the small visitor center, located at the far end of Luluku Rd, over 1 mile *mauka* (inland) from the Kamehameha Hwy. Call ahead to register for free two-hour guided nature walks (10am Saturday and 1pm Sunday). (☑808-233-7323; www.honolulu.gov/parks/hbg.html; 45-680 Luluku Rd; admission free; ⊙9am-4pm)

He'eia Pier

HARBOR

9 ◎ Map p114, B1

Just north of, and run in conjunction with, the state park is one of the Windward Coast's only small boat harbors. It's fun just to watch the comings and goings of local boat owners. On weekends they head out to the 'sandbar,' a raised spit in the bay that becomes a mooring party place for people to kick back and relax.

Kawai Nui Marsh

PARK

10 ◎ Map p114, E2

One of Hawaii's largest fresh-water marshes, Kawai Nui provides flood protection for the town, a habitat for endangered waterbirds, and is also one of the largest remaining fishponds used by ancient Hawaiians. You may see rare birds including the *koloa maoli* (Hawaiian duck), *ae'o* (Hawaiian stilt), *'alae kea* (Hawaiian coot) and *kolea* (Pacific golden plover). Several local groups work to preserve and restore the marsh. To access the area, park in the lot at the end of Kaha St, off Oneawa St, just over a mile northwest of Kailua Rd. (www.kawainuimarsh.com; off Kaha St; admission free; ⊙7am-7pm)

Hamakua Marsh Wildlife Sanctuary

WILDLIFE RESERVE

11 ◎ Map p114, E3

Downstream from Kawai Nui Marsh, this tiny nature preserve provides more habitat for rare waterbirds, including the *koloa maoli* (Hawaiian duck), *ae'o* (Hawaiian black-necked stilt), *'alae ke'oke'o* (Hawaiian coot) and *'alae 'ula* (Hawaiian moorhen). Bird-watching is best after heavy rains. To keep these endangered birds wild, do not feed

> ## Understand
> ### Kailua vs Kane'ohe
>
> A long, graceful bay protected by a coral reef is Kailua's claim to fame. The nearly 4-mile-long shoreline stretch of ivory sand is made for strolling, and the weather and wave conditions can be just about perfect for swimming, kayaking, windsurfing and kitesurfing. None of this has gone unnoticed. Decades ago expatriates from the mainland bought up cottages crowded into the little neighborly lanes; the ones near the beachfront were often replaced with mega-houses. South along the shore lies the exclusive enclave of Lanikai, with million-dollar views – and mansions that may be valued at 10 times that much.
>
> The state's largest bay and reef-sheltered lagoon, Kane'ohe Bay is largely silted and not great for swimming. The town itself is a Marine-base suburb, populated by chain restaurants and stores. It just doesn't pack the eating and sleeping appeal of neighboring town Kailua, which is only 6 miles (15 minutes) south.

them. Park off Hamakua Dr, behind Down to Earth natural-foods store. (http://hawaii.gov/dlnr/; off Hamakua Dr; admission free; ☉sunrise-sunset)

Akebono Statue STATUE

 12 ◉ Map p114, F5

Posed in fighting form, outside East Honolulu Clothing Company in Waimanalo Town Center, is one of Waimanolo's most famous sons. Chad Rowan was born here in 1969 and went on to make history by becoming the first non-Japanese-born sumo wrestler ever to reach *yokozuna*, the highest rank in sumo. At 6ft 8in (203cm) in height and a hefty 514lb (233kg) in weight, Akebono (as Chad was known in the ring) was a *yokozuna* for eight years, winning 11 championships before his retirement in 2001.

Eating

Tamura's Poke SEAFOOD $

 13 🍴 Map p114, E2

The wine is fine, but you're really here for the *poke*. Tucked into the back of Tamura's Fine Wines & Liquors is a deli with a top *poke* selection. Some say this is the best on the island! (☎808-254-2000; www.tamurasfinewine.com; 25 Kane'ohe Bay Dr; per lb $7-15; ☉10:30am-7:45pm)

Whole Foods SUPERMARKET $

 14 🍴 Map p114, H2

Emphasizing organic, natural and locally sourced food, this supermarket offers deliciously healthy options. Grab a hot meal from the full-service deli – sandwiches, BBQ meats or tacos, anyone? – or graze the pizza, *poke*, sushi and salad bars. Island-made gelato is sold at the coffee kiosk up front. Come for happy-hour drinks and *pupu* at the supermarket's Windward Bar. (☏808-263-6800; http://wholefoods market.com/stores/kailua; Kailua Town Center, 629 Kailua Rd; ☺7am-10pm; ☏)

Rai Rai Ramen
JAPANESE $

15 Map p114, F1

Look for the red-and-white banner written in kanji outside this brightly lit noodle shop. The menu of ramen styles ranges from Sapporo south to Hakata, all with rich broth and topped with tender pork, if you like. The *gyōza* (dumplings) are grilled or steamed bundles of heaven. (☏808-230-8208; 124 Oneawa St; mains $7-10; ☺11am-8:30pm Wed-Mon)

Serg's Mexican Kitchen Nalo
MEXICAN $

16 Map p114, G5

Whether you're heading to the beach or are cruising on a round-island trip, Serg's offers an excellent roadside

Top Tip

Golf Anyone?

LPGA star Michelle Wie got her start here, and President Obama often swings through **Olomana Golf Links** (Map p114, F4; ☏808-259-7926; www.pacificlinks.com/olomana; 41-1801 Kalaniana'ole Hwy; green fees $100) on his holidays. This 18-hole, par-72 course beneath the dramatic backdrop of the Ko'olau Range also has a driving range and restaurant.

option for takeout or eat-in Mexican favorites. Try the fish tacos. (☏808-259-7374; 41-865 Kalaniana'ole Hwy; mains $6-11; ☺10am-8pm)

Sweet Home Waimanalo
HAWAIIAN

17 Map p114, G5

Taste local Waimanalo's back-to-the-earth farm goodness from this family kitchen, where local chicken gets sauced with honey and citrus, and fresh corn tortillas wrap lime cream and grilled fish for tacos. Even the island standards get a twist: the *kalua* pork sandwich is topped with bok choy slaw. (☏808-259-5737; http://sweethome waimanalo.com; 41-1025 Kalaniana'ole Hwy; mains $8-13; ☺9:30am-6.30pm Wed-Mon)

Tersty Treats
SEAFOOD $

18 Map p114, F5

This locally owned fish market lets you sample a dozen different flavors of freshly made *poke,* including old-school luau tastes like crab, squid and *opihi* (Hawaiian limpet). Keep filling up your beach cooler with deli faves like *char siu* pork and seared ahi belly. (☏808-259-3474; 41-1540 Kalaniana'ole Hwy; mains $6-12; ☺10am-7pm Mon-Thu, 10am-8pm Fri & Sat, 10am-5pm Sun)

Kalapawai Cafe
BISTRO, DELI $$

19 Map p114, F2

A gourmet, self-serve deli by day, after 5pm it transforms into an inviting, eclectic bistro. The eggplant bruschetta

Hawaiian specialty *ahi poke* (cubed, marinated yellowfin or bigeye tuna)

and other share dishes are excellent paired with a wine flight (a series of tasting-sized pours). But it's hard to resist the creative, ingredient-driven mains. Dine streetside on the lanai or in the intimate candlelit dining room. (☏808-262-2354; www.kalapawaimarket.com/section/cafe; 750 Kailua Rd; dinner mains $14-24; ⏱6am-9pm Mon-Thu, to 9:30pm Fri & Sat, from 7am Sun)

Cinnamon's Restaurant
BREAKFAST $$

21 ✖ Map p114, H1

Locals pack this family cafe decorated like Grandma's house for the airy chiffon pancakes drowning in guava syrup, Portuguese sweet-bread French toast, eggs Benedict mahimahi, curried-chicken-and-papaya salad, and Hawaiian plate lunches. Waits are long on weekends; only the breakfast menu is available Sunday. (☏808-261-8724; www.cinnamons808.com; Kailua Sq, 315 Uluniu St; mains $7-13; ⏱7am-2pm; 👶)

Tokuname Sushi Bar & Restaurant
JAPANESE $$

21 ✖ Map p114, G1

Surprisingly good sushi considering the suburban location in Kailua. Daily early-bird and late-night sushi power hour (9pm to 10pm) specials help keep the costs down, too. (☏808-262-8656; www.tokonamehawaii.com; 442 Uluniu St; sushi $5-10, dinner mains $10-16; ⏱4-11pm)

Local Life
Kalapawai Market

A don't-miss 1930s landmark market near Kailua Beach, **Kalapawai Market** (Map p114, F3; www.kalapawaimarket.com; 306 S Kalaheo Ave; items $2-12; ⏱6am-9pm) stocks picnic supplies and serves the same fancy, made-to-order sandwiches and market-fresh salads as its in-town sister. Good coffee, too. Get your supplies and wander around to the beach.

Baci Bistro
ITALIAN $$

22 Map p114, H1

Home-grown Italian cooking, where the owner knows most patrons by name. Don't miss the white chocolate mascarpone cheesecake. The ravioli is made fresh daily. (www.bacibistro.com; 30 Aulike St; mains lunch $10-15, dinner $15-25; ⏱11:30am-2pm & 5:30-10pm Mon-Fri, 5:30-10pm Sat & Sun)

Buzz's
STEAK $$$

23 Map p114, F3

Classic mainlander expat territory; beachfront home-owning regulars here definitely get the best service. But the old-school kitschy island decor, surf-and-turf menu (complete with throwback salad bar) and proximity to the beach make it worth the stop. Book ahead, but still expect a wait. (☎808-261-4661; http://buzzsoriginalsteakhouse.com; 413 Kawailoa Rd; mains lunch $9-17, dinner $16-38; ⏱11am-3pm & 4:30-9:30pm)

Drinking

Lanikai Juice
HEALTH FOOD $

24 Map p114, H2

With fresh fruit grown by local farmers getting blended and poured into biodegradable cups, this juice bar makes addictive smoothies with names like Going Bananas and Lanikai Splash. In the morning, neighborhood yoga fanatics devour overflowing bowls of granola topped with acai berries, apple bananas and grated coconut at sunny sidewalk tables. (☎262-2383; www.lanikaijuice.com; Kailua Shopping Center, 600 Kailua Rd; snacks & drinks $4-8; ⏱6am-8pm Mon-Fri, 7am-7pm Sat & Sun)

Morning Brew Coffee House & Bistro
CAFE

25 Map p114, H2

Baristas at this pleasant cafe cup everything from chai to 'Funky Monkey' mochas with banana syrup. Swing by for an espresso or for bagel breakfasts, hot-pressed panini lunches and ahi tuna kebabs and wine at dinner. (☎808-262-7770; http://morningbrewhawaii.com; Kailua Shopping Center, 600 Kailua Rd; ⏱6am-8pm Tue-Sat, to 7pm Sun & Mon; 🛜)

Kailua Town Pub & Grill
PUB

26 Map p114, G2

This casual Irish pub wannabe has tasty from-scratch Bloody Marys, sports on the TV and a friendly mixed-age crowd. Best burgers in town too, not to mention the fish and chips. (☎808-230-8444; http://kailuatownpub.com; 26 Hoʻolai St; ⏱10am-2am Mon-Sat, 7am-2am Sun)

Shopping

Kailua
Shopping Center   GIFTS, BOOKS

27 🔒 Map p114, H2

Start your souvenir shopping downtown at this strip mall opposite Macy's department store. Pick up Hawaiiana books and beach reads at **Bookends** (⏰9am-8pm Mon-Sat, to 5pm Sun), tropically scented lotions and soaps at **Lanikai Bath & Body** (⏰10am-6pm Mon-Fri, to 5pm Sat, to 4pm Sun) or beachy home accents, tote bags and kids' toys at **Sand People** (⏰10am-6pm Mon-Sat, to 5pm Sun). (600 Kailua Rd)

Madre Chocolate   FOOD & DRINK

28 🔒 Map p114, F2

Aficionados will be wowed by these award-winning Hawaiian-made boutique chocolates infused with island flavors – coconut and caramelized ginger, passion fruit, kiawe-smoked sea salt. Kailua is home, but there's a new store in Honolulu's Chinatown. (📞808-377-6440; http://madrechocolate.com; 20-A Kainehe St; ⏰11am-7pm Tue-Fri, to 6pm Sat)

Lily Lotus   CLOTHING

29 🔒 Map p114, H2

Outfit for the yoga lifestyle with breathable and organic clothing from a Honolulu-local designer. You can also buy mats, jewelry and accessories by Lily and other makers. (📞808-888-3564; www.lilylotus.com; Suite 102, 609 Kailua Rd; ⏰10am-6pm Mon-Sat, 11am-4pm Sun)

East Honolulu Clothing
Company   CLOTHING, SOUVENIRS

30 🔒 Map p114, F5

The striking, graphic one-color tropical prints on the clothing here are all designed and silk screened in-house. This company provides many local hula schools with their costumes. There's plenty of local artwork to peruse as well. (www.doublepawswear.com; Waimanalo Town Shopping Center, 41-537 Kalaniana'ole Hwy; ⏰9am-5pm)

Naturally Hawaiian
Gallery   ARTS, CRAFTS

Since it shares space inside a converted gas station with Sweet Home Waimanalo (see 17 ❌ Map p114, G5), you can browse island artists' paintings and handmade crafts while you wait for a kale smoothie. Naturalist Patrick Ching's prints are especially good. (www.patrickchingart.com; 41-1025 Kalaniana'ole Hwy; ⏰9:30am-5:30pm)

Waimanalo Market Co-op   MARKET

A local co-operative selling everything from art to kitchenware to fruit and vegetables. Next to Sweet Home Waimanalo (see 17 ❌ Map p114, G5). (📞808-690-0390; www.waimanalomarket.com; 41-1029 Kalaniana'ole Hwy; ⏰9am-6pm Thu-Sun)

The Best of
Honolulu

Honolulu's Best Walks

Honolulu's Best...

Waikiki Beach (p76) at night
M SWEET / GETTY IMAGES ©

Best Walks
Historical Honolulu

🏃 The Walk

Honolulu's Historical District is so compact that it's easy to take your time and still inspect all the major sites in a day. There's a lot of intriguing history and art packed into a small area that is right next to Downtown's tall buildings and only a 10-minute walk away from Chinatown. Enjoy this walk at your leisure – it could take anything from one hour to an entire day.

Start 'Iolani Palace

Finish Mission Houses Museum

Length 1.5 miles; 2 hours

✕ Take a Break

Drop into the downstairs cafe at the Hawai'i State Art Museum or head down Richards Ave to **Cafe Julia** (p38).

State Capitol (p30)

❶ 'Iolani Palace

Start your walk at the impressive **'Iolani Palace** (p24). The palace was built under King David Kalakaua in 1882, and the grounds are open during daylight hours and are free of charge. Head *mauka* (towards the mountains) to find the **Queen Lili'uokalani Statue** (p25).

❷ State Capitol

Built in the '60s, Hawaii's **State Capitol** (p30) takes conceptual postmodernism to a new level. If you want to take a self-guided tour, head to Room 415 and grab a brochure. Out front on Beretania St, check out the stylized **Father Damien Statue** (p30).

❸ Washington Place

Over the road, **Washington Place** (p32) was formerly the governor's official residence. This colonial-style mansion was built in 1846. Admire it from the street before crossing Richards St.

❹ Hawai'i State Art Museum

With its vibrant, thought-provoking collections, the **Hawai'i State Art Museum** (p30) brings together traditional and contemporary art from Hawaii's multiethnic communities in a grand 1928 Spanish Mission Revival–style building.

❺ Ali'iolani Hale

You'll know you're at the right place by the impressive **Kamehameha the Great Statue** (p31) out front.

The **Ali'iolani Hale** (p30), the 'House of Heavenly Kings' was built in 1874 and today houses the Supreme Court of Hawai'i. Take a look at the informative **King Kamehameha V Judiciary History Center**.

❻ Kawaiaha'o Church

Nicknamed 'Westminster Abbey of the Pacific,' **Kawaiaha'o Church** (p31) was built in 1842 in New England Gothic–style of 14,000 coral slabs. Don't miss the **tomb of King**

Lunalilo out front, or the **small cemetery** to the rear of the church, which is almost like a who's who of local colonial history.

❼ Mission Houses Museum

The **Mission Houses Museum** (p32) occupies the original headquarters of the Sandwich Islands mission, which forever changed the course of Hawaiian history. You'll need to take a guided tour to peek inside any of the buildings.

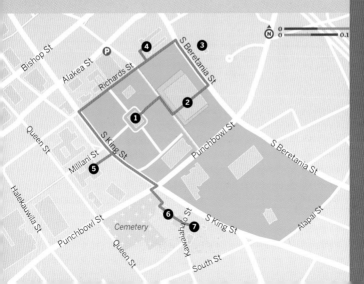

Best Walks
Waikiki Wander

🏃 The Walk

You're in for a bit of history and hedonism on this wander through Waikiki. History, as in a visit to the Hawai'i Army Museum and perusals of statues of Hawaiian legends, and hedonism, as in some time on the beach and strolling into two of Waikiki's oldest luxury hotels.

Start King David Kalakaua Statue

Finish Prince Kuhio Statue

Length 1.5 miles; two hours

✖ Take a Break

You'll be up for a break at the **Royal Hawaiian Center** (Map p74, D3; www.royalhawaiiancenter.com; 2201 Kalakaua Ave; ⏱10am-10pm). There's a good food court on the 2nd floor of Bldg B, and if you're ready for a cold one, **Five-O Bar & Lounge** (p85) is right there.

Kayaks for rent, Fort DeRussy Beach (p76)

LINDA CHING / GETTY IMAGES ©

❶ King David Kalakaua Statue

The **King David Kalakaua statue** (p78) greets visitors coming into Waikiki on the road named after the man himself. Born in 1836, King Kalakaua ruled Hawaii from 1874 until his death in 1891.

❷ Hawai'i Army Museum

The **Hawai'i Army Museum** (p80) showcases military paraphernalia as it relates to Hawaii's history, starting with shark-tooth clubs that Kamehameha the Great used to win control of the island more than two centuries ago.

❸ Fort DeRussy Beach

Seldom crowded, **Fort DeRussy Beach** (p76) extends along the shore. Beach-hut concessionaires rent bodyboards, kayaks and snorkel sets. When you're ready, head towards Diamond Head along the beach.

❹ Royal Hawaiian Hotel

Head in through the Sheraton Waikiki to the

Royal Hawaiian Hotel (p79). This gorgeously restored 1927 art-deco landmark is dubbed the 'Pink Palace.' Carry on out to the **Royal Hawaiian Center** (p128) on Kalakaua Ave.

❺ Moana Surfrider Hotel

Browse your way down Kalakaua Ave to the **Moana Surfrider Hotel** (p79). Opened in 1901, this plantation-style inn was once the haunt of Hollywood movie stars, aristocrats and business tycoons.

❻ Kahaloa & Ulukou Beaches

Waikiki's busiest section of sand and surf, **Kahaloa & Ulukou Beaches** (p77) are great for sunbathing, swimming and people-watching. Consider a 1.5-hour cruise on the **Na Hoku II Catamaran** (p78).

❼ Duke Kahanamoku Statue

Just past the Waikiki Police Station and the **Wizard Stones of Kapaemahu** (p78), admire the **Duke Kahan-amoku Statue** (p89). Duke is considered the 'father of modern surfing' and a Waikiki legend.

❽ Prince Kuhio Statue

Admire the **Prince Kuhio Statue** (p71). Kuhio was prince when the Kingdom of Hawaii was overthrown in 1893. He later became Hawaii's congressional delegate for 10 consecutive terms. Have a swim at **Kuhio Beach Park** (p70).

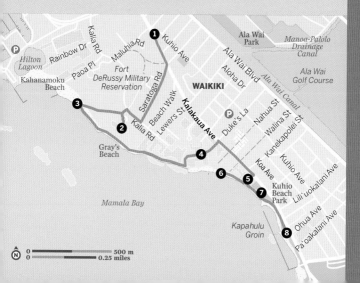

Best
Beaches

Think of Hawaii, and you're instantly dreaming about golden sands backed by tropical palm trees, right? Well, the good news is that you'll be spoiled for choice! When it comes to coastal strands, swimming beaches come in a rainbow of hues and water temperatures are idyllic. You can usually find somewhere to swim, no matter the season.

When & Where

Take a look at a map of O'ahu. The eastern coast is called the Windward Coast, as, year-round, northeasterly Trade Winds make this the windy side of the island. The west coast, in the lee of the mountains, has less wind and is known as the Leeward Coast. In winter, ocean swells arrive from the north, meaning great surf on the North Shore and good swimming on the South Shore and Waikiki. In summer, it's the opposite. Ocean swells arrive from the south, bringing waves into Waikiki and turning the North Shore into a pond.

Facilities & The Law

Most of Hawaii's state and county beach parks have basic restrooms and outdoor cold-water showers; about half are patrolled by lifeguards. By law, all beaches are open to the public below the high-tide line. Nudity is legally prohibited on public beaches.

Don't Get Stung!

Jellyfish turn up eight to 10 days after the full moon each month; this is not a good time to be in the water. Check on www.to-hawaii.com/jellyfish calendar.html for dates. If you do get stung – and it's painful! – talk to the lifeguard immediately.

MAKENA STOCK MEDIA / GETTY IMAGES ©

Best South Shore Beaches

Ala Moana Beach Park
Broad, golden-sand beach opposite the Ala Moana shopping mall. (p49)

Kahanamoku Beach
Fronting the Hilton Hawaiian Village at the western end of Waikiki. (p76)

Kahaloa & Ulukou Beaches Waikiki's busiest section of sand. (p77)

Kuhio Beach Park
The heart of the action in Waikiki with Duke's statue and hula shows. (p70)

Kapi'olani Beach Park Popular with local families in weekends. (p77)

Sans Souci Beach Park
Locals call it Kaimana Beach and hang out here. (p78)

Lanikai Beach (p116)

Hanauma Bay Legendary top snorkeling spot in an ancient volcanic crater. (p106)

Sandy Beach Park One for watching only unless you're a pro bodyboarder. (p109)

Best Windward Coast Beaches

Waimanalo Bay Beach Park A beauty with great waves for novice bodyboarders. (p116)

Bellows Field Beach Park Fine sand fronting Bellows Air Force Station. (p116)

Kailua Beach Park Ideal for leisurely walks and aquatic activities. (p116)

Lanikai Beach Gorgeous stretch of powdery white sand backed by millionaires' mansions. (p116)

 Worth a Trip

On O'ahu's **North Shore**, but barely an hour's drive from Honolulu, are some of the world's best known surfing beaches. Things really pump in winter at **Sunset Beach**, **Pipeline** and **Waimea Bay** – the **Triple Crown of Surfing** (www.vanstriplecrownof surfing.com) is a spectacular event from late November to early December.

Best
Eating

ANN CECIL / GETTY IMAGES ©

Forget about pineapple upside-down cake and tiki-bar cocktails. 'Dis is seriously broke da mout!' That's the ultimate compliment you'll hear if you hang around locals long enough. It means something is so delicious it breaks the mouth. And that's no exaggeration. People go crazy over food. So, be brave and eat everything in sight. It's all *'ono grinds* (good eats).

Informal Dining

Informal dining is Hawaii's forte. For local food and rock-bottom prices, swing by retro drive-ins and diners with Formica tables, open from morning till night. Portion sizes can be gigantic, so feel free to split a meal or take home leftovers, like locals do. The casual Hawaii dress code means T-shirts and flip-flops are ubiquitous, except at Honolulu's most up-scale restaurants and Waikiki's luxury resort hotels.

Open from *pau hana* (happy hour) until late, most bars serve tasty *pupu* (appetizers or small shared plates) like *poke*, shrimp tempura or eda-mame (boiled soybeans in the pod).

Gourmet Cuisine

For gourmet cuisine by Hawaii's star chefs, explore Honolulu. Hawaii's cutting-edge foodie trends all start in the capital city. Hawaii Regional Cuisine (HRC) is hallmarked by Asian and Pacific Rim fusion tastes, yet remains upscale, usually found in beach-resort restaurants and celebrity chef's kitchens.

Self-catering

For groceries, head to farmers markets and locally owned supermarkets. In Hawaii, most groceries are imported. The everyday price of food averages 30% more than on the US mainland, so you may not save much money by cooking your own meals.

Best Local Food

Kaka'ako Kitchen
Healthy minded plate lunches. (p49)

Rainbow Drive-In
The best in local plate-lunches and dinners. (p73)

Sweet Home Waimanalo Farm goodness from a family kitchen. (p120)

Best Gourmet Cuisine

Alan Wong's Creative interpretations of Hawaiian Regional Cuisine. (p53)

Cafe Julia Elegant cuisine in an open-air setting. (p38)

Malasadas (Portugese fried doughnuts) from Leonard's

Best Fusion

The Pig & the Lady One of the hottest new places on the island. (p37)

Uncle Bo's Pupu Bar & Grill Fusion *pupu* crafted with flair. (📞808-735-8311; www.unclebosrestaurant. com; 559 Kapahulu Ave, Waikiki; 🕐5pm-1am)

Best Sweets

Leonard's Serving legendary *malasadas* since the 1950s. (📞808-737-5591; www.leonards hawaii.com; 933 Kapahulu Ave, Waikiki; 🕐5:30am-10pm Sun-Thu, 5:30am-11pm Fri & Sat)

Bubbies Nothing beats *mochi* ice-cream. (p111)

◈ Worth a Trip

Walking through the door is like stepping into another era at **Helena's Hawaiian Food** (📞808-845-8044; http://helenas hawaiianfood.com; 1240 N School St; 🕐10am-7:30pm Tue-Fri). Even though long-time owner Helena Chock has passed away, her relatives still command the family kitchen, which opened in 1946. Most people order à la carte and Helena's is good!

Best
Drinking & Entertainment

There is so much going on in Honolulu that it's hard to keep up. In general, locals party in the edgy art and nightlife scene of Chinatown, while tourists and those more in the mainstream stick close to Waikiki's golden sands and golden mile. There's not much in the way of nightlife in Kahala, Hawai'i Kai or Kailua.

Bars, Lounges & Nightclubs

Every self-respecting bar has a *pupu* menu to complement the liquid sustenance, and some bars are as famous for their appetizers as their good times atmosphere. A key term to know is *pau hana* (literally 'stop work'), Hawaiian pidgin for 'happy hour.'

Almost all of the hip bars and nightclubs have migrated to Chinatown.

Live Music

If Hawaiian music is what you crave, don't look any further than Waikiki. But if it's jazz, alt-rock and punk sounds you're after, venture outside the tourist zone into Honolulu's other neighborhoods.

Hawaii's capital city is also home to a symphony orchestra, an opera company, ballet troupes, chamber orchestras and more, while more than a dozen community theater groups perform everything from David Mamet satires to Hawaiian pidgin fairy tales.

Hawaiian Music & Hula

Traditional and contemporary Hawaiian music calls all up and down the beach in Waikiki, from the rhythmic drums and *ipu* (gourds) accompanying *hula* dancers to mellow duos or trios playing slack key guitars and ukuleles and singing with *leo ki'eki'e* (male) or *ha'i* (female) high falsetto voices. Luau shows are Waikiki-based.

LINDA CHING / GETTY IMAGES ©

☑ **Top Tip**

For what's going on this week, from live-music and DJ gigs to theater, movies and cultural events, check the **Honolulu Star-Advertiser's TGIF** (www.honolulupulse.com) and the free **Honolulu Weekly** (http://honolulu-weekly.com).

Best Bars, Lounges & Nightclubs

RumFire Lively bar at the Sheraton Waikiki. (p84)

Kona Brewing Company Hawaiian brews out in Hawai'i Kai. (p111)

Kailua Town Pub & Grill Relaxed atmosphere in Kailua. (p122)

Hula performance, House Without a Key (p88)

Best Live Music

Dragon Upstairs Jazz and blues in Chinatown. (p40)

Republik The city's most intimate concert venue. (p56)

Jazz Minds Art & Café Top island talent in speakeasy ambience. (p56)

Best Hawaiian Music & Hula

House Without a Key Open-air lounge beneath old kiawe tree. (p88)

Mai Tai Bar The Royal Hawaiian's low-key bar. (p88)

'Aha 'Aina Top luau and show in Waikiki. (p90)

Best Performing Arts

Hawaii Theatre Major venue for dance, music and theater. (p27)

Kumu Kahua Theatre Dedicated to works by Hawaiian playwrights. (p42)

Diamond Head Theatre Third-oldest running community theater in the US. (p103)

Best
Museums

Your prime purpose for coming to O'ahu may be the beach, but the city offers up some stunning museums and art museums that are well worth your time. Polynesian, Pearl Harbor and pioneering history is all on display, while the city's art museums are first class and may be the highlights of your trip.

MICK ELMORE / GETTY IMAGES ©

Museums

Bishop Museum One of the world's top Polynesian anthropological museums; like Hawaii's version of the Smithsonian Institute. (p61)

'Iolani Palace The Hawaiian royal palace restored to its former glory; no other place evokes a more poignant sense of Hawaii's history. (p24)

WWII Valor in the Pacific National Monument Pearl Harbor historic sites and museums;

a solemn tribute to those who lost their lives at Pearl Harbor. (p65)

Mission Houses Museum The stories of the Protestant missionaries at the original headquarters of the Sandwich Islands mission. (p32)

Hawai'i Army Museum Showcases military paraphernalia relating to Hawaii. (p80)

Art Museums

Honolulu Museum of Art This exceptional fine-arts museum could

be the biggest surprise of your trip to O'ahu. (p46)

Honolulu Museum of Art at Spalding House Meditative sculpture and art high above Honolulu; magnificent views. (p47)

Hawai'i State Art Museum Vibrant, thought-provoking collections; art from Hawaii's multiethnic communities. (p30)

Shangri La Doris Duke's spectacular sanctuary and Islamic art out past Diamond Head. (p98)

Best
Hawaiiana
Shopping

LINDA CHING / GETTY IMAGES ©

Something authentic from the islands rather than a head-bobbing dashboard hula doll from an ABC Store in Waikiki? The stores listed have the best in Hawaiiana, that special something representing the multicultural Hawaii that we know today – quality antiques, handicrafts, ukeleles, fabric, aloha shirts and more. Get something special from O'ahu to take home.

Native Books/Nā Mea Hawaii Hawaiian handicrafts, music, souvenirs and cultural classes. (p49)

Cindy's Lei Shoppe Crafted flower lei in Chinatown. (p42)

Kamaka Hawaii Handcrafted ukeleles since 1916; original shapes. (p42)

Manuheali'i Bold and original island clothing designs. (p57)

Tin Can Mailman Thoughtfully collected Hawaiiana treasures and antiques in Chinatown. (p42)

Bailey's Antiques & Aloha Shirts The ultimate in aloha shirt collections; thousands to choose from. (p73)

Na Lima Mili Hulu No'eau Makers of traditional feather lei. (p92)

Ukulele PuaPua Tops for ukeleles in Waikiki; free lessons daily. (p92)

Naturally Hawaiian Gallery Paintings and crafts in Waimanalo. (p123)

Gyotaku by Naoki Fabulous fish prints in Kane'ohe; watch them being made. (p118)

Best
Festivals & Events

Chinese New Year (http://chinatown honolulu.org) Chinatown's lunar new year festivities in late January and early February.

Duke Kahanamoku Challenge Canoe and paddleboard races in late February.

Honolulu Festival (www.honolulufestival.com) Cultural performances and parade in mid-March.

'I Love Kailua' Town Party Community block party in Kaiua in April.

Waikiki Spam Jam (www.spamjamhawaii.com) Street festival to celebrate everyone's favorite canned-meat product, Spam, in late April.

Mele Mei (www.melemei.com) Month-long celebration of Hawaiian music in May.

Lantern Floating Hawaii Japanese floating-lantern ceremony on the last Monday in May.

Pan-Pacific Festival (www.pan-pacific-festival.com) A monster party celebrating everything Pacific and Asian in early June.

King Kamehameha Hula Competition Huge hula festival in late June.

Prince Lot Hula Festival Non-competitive hula event on the third Saturday in July.

Na Hula Festival Music and dance celebrations at Waikiki Shell in early August.

Hawaiian Slack Key Guitar Festival (www.slackkeyfestival.com) At Kaiolani Park in mid-August.

Hawai'i Food & Wine Festival (www.hawaiifoodandwinefestival.com) Long weekend of wining and dining in early September.

Aloha Festivals (www.alohafestivals.com) Statewide cultural festivals in September.

Hawaii International Film Festival (www.hiff.org) Massive film festival in late October and early November.

DANITA DELIMONT / GETTY IMAGES ©

☑ **Top Tip**

Waikiki loves to party year-round. Every Friday night, usually starting around 7:45pm, the Hilton Hawaiian Village shoots off a big ol' **fireworks show**, visible from beachside Waikiki. A top spot to watch from is Magic Island in Ala Moana Beach Park.

King Kalakaua's Birthday Concert by the Royal Hawaiian Band on November 16.

Pearl Harbor Day Commemoration and Hawaiian Blessing at Pearl Harbor (December 7).

Honolulu Marathon (www.honolulumarathon.org) On the second Sunday of December.

Best
For Kids

The beach may well be enough to keep kids entertained for much of the day, but it pays to have a few more options up your sleeve. In particular, Waikiki is very family-friendly. Outdoor activities range call from the water to the mountains, while if the weather turns bad, head indoors to the treasure-trove that is Bishop Museum.

INTI ST CLAIR / GETTY IMAGES ©

Bishop Museum Children love the Science Adventure Center's multimedia exhibits and the planetarium. (p61)

Manoa Falls Trail Short, family-friendly hike to a waterfall. (p63)

Ala Moana Centertainment Movies at the Ala Moana Center. (p56)

Waikiki Aquarium Fun with tropical fish, including family events and educational programs. (p79)

Honolulu Zoo Petting zoo, 'twilight tours' and other options for kids. (p80)

Kuhio Beach Park Learn to surf or outrigger-canoe; great introduction to the water for toddlers. (p70)

Kahala Mall Movies and shopping in Kahala. (p103)

Diamond Head Family adventure! Climb Diamond Head. (p96)

Hanauma Bay World-class snorkeling spot for kids. (p106)

Waimanalo Bay Beach Park Top spot for swimming and learning to bodyboard. (p116)

☑ **Top Tip**

Two freebies in Waikiki that the kids will love are the year-round Friday night **fireworks show** (7.45pm), easily seen from Waikiki beaches, and the **Torch Lighting & Hula Show** at Kuhio Beach held Tuesday, Thursday and Saturday nights from 6.30pm (6pm in winter).

Best
Outdoor Activities

Honolulu is a dream destination for those keen to get outside. Here you can hike sandy beaches, or climb up into the mountains for a forest trek. Go for a simple snorkel or an all-day scuba dive. Island-wide opportunities for swimming, kayaking, stand-up paddling and more abound. Oh, and did we mention there's some pretty decent surfing?

DONALD MIRALLE / GETTY IMAGES ©

In or on Water

If you want to get wet, here is a non-exhaustive list of options for your consideration: swimming, snorkeling, bodysurfing and bodyboarding, surfing, stand-up paddling, kayaking, kitesurfing and windsurfing, outrigger canoeing, diving, boating, fishing, whale-watching... Shall we go on?

On the Land

Nature sits right outside Honolulu's door. About 25% of the island is protected natural areas and the lush mountainous interior is carved by hiking trails. Consider hiking, cycling and mountain biking, camping, horseback riding, running, golf and tennis.

In the Air

Think kitesurfing and paragliding, though Dillingham Airfield on the North Shore offers parachuting, gliding, ultralights and biplane rides – and is less than an hour's drive from Waikiki.

Best Water Activities

Hanauma Bay Snorkeling and diving paradise! (p106)

Kuhio Beach Park Learn to surf or outrigger-canoe! (p70)

Kailua Beach Park Paddle kayaks to offshore islands; learn to kitesurf. (p116)

☑ **Top Tip**

If camping is your thing, there are great options on O'ahu. Advance permits required – check out **Honolulu Department of Parks & Recreation** (https://camping.honolulu.gov) and **Hawaii Division of State Parks** (www.hawaii stateparks.org).

Best Land Activities

Diamond Head Climb Waikiki's famous backdrop. (p96)

Manoa Falls Trail Hike into the lush mountainous interior. (p63)

Waimanalo Bay Beach Park Camp beside the waves. (p116)

Best
Hikes

O'ahu's interior is lush, making for enjoyable hiking. Climb up high and you'll be rewarded with stupendous views, stick to the valleys and you'll love the tropical vegetation. You'll need sturdy footwear as it often gets muddy, but there are no snakes or poisonous plants, nor many wild animals. Use common sense when it comes to the changeable weather.

Geography

The island of O'ahu is really two separate shield volcanoes that arose about two million years ago and formed two mountain ranges: Wai'anae in the northwest and Ko'olau in the southeast. O'ahu's last gasp of volcanic activity occurred over 10,000 years ago and created the tuff cone of Diamond Head, O'ahu's most famous geographical landmark. The forces of erosion – wind, rain and waves – subsequently added more geologic character, cutting valleys, creating beaches and turning a mound of lava into paradise.

Diamond Head 1.6-mile return hike up stairs and through tunnels to amazing views. (p97)

Manoa Falls Trail Rewarding 1.6-mile round-trip trail to the falls. (p63)

Nu'uanu Valley Lookout A 5.5-mile return hike to high atop the Ko'olau Range. (p63)

Kuli'ou'ou Ridge Trail Climbs to fine views above Hawai'i Kai; 5-mile round-trip. (p110)

Koko Crater Trail Steep climb straight up an extinct volcano. (p110)

Makapu'u Point Lighthouse Trail A 2-mile return trip on a paved road to the lighthouse; great views. (p110)

CHRISTINA LEASE / GETTY IMAGES ©

☑ Top Tip

▶ For more hiking trails island-wide, visit **Na Ala Hele Hawaii Trail & Access System** (http://hawaiitrails.ehawaii.gov).

▶ For group hikes, check the **Honolulu Weekly** (http://honoluluweekly.com) calendar, **Hawaiian Trail & Mountain Club** (http://htmclub.org) and **Sierra Club** (www.hi.sierraclub.org/oahu).

▶ For guided walks, look at **Hiking Hawaii** (hiking hawaii808.com).

Best
Shopping Centers

If shopping rocks your world, there are plenty of opportunities everywhere you look in Honolulu. While most visitors do their shopping in Waikiki or at Ala Moana, there are a number of other shopping centers that may be worth your time, from the Ward complexes to suburban Kahala, Hawai'i Kai and Kailua.

ANN CECIL / GETTY IMAGES ©

Waikiki Shopping

On beachfront Kalakaua Ave, Waikiki's shopping centers are mostly chock-full of brand-label stores you'd find in any US mainland city. A handful of only-in-Hawaii stores line Waikiki Beach Walk. For offbeat, vintage and antique, and one-of-a-kind shops, walk inland along Kuhio Ave and locals' Kapahulu Ave.

Going & Coming

Waikiki's atmospheric old International Marketplace is gone, soon to be replaced by a massive new shopping center.

Aloha Marketplace has been bought by Hawaii Pacific University and is being revitalized for retail, dining and student housing. And Sears is gone from the Ala Moana Center, where huge expansion is going on.

Ala Moana Center
Largest open-air shopping center in the world. (p49)

Ward Warehouse
Mini-mall has many one-of-a-kind island shops. (p56)

Royal Hawaiian Center
Waikiki's biggest shopping center. (p128)

☑ **Top Tip**

The mother-lode in terms of outlet stores, **Waikele Premium Outlets**, is west of Pearl Harbor. It's so popular that there is direct transport from Waikiki.

Kahala Mall Neighborhood mall with good mix of only-in-Hawaii shops. (p103)

Kailua Shopping Center A bit of everything in downtown Kailua. (p123)

Best
Gardens, Sanctuaries & Cemeteries

There are ample opportunities to check out O'ahu's various ecosystems from the lush and wet interior vegetation such as at Lyon Arboretum in the Upper Manoa Valley, to the arid and the dry at Koko Crater Botanical Garden. Two well-known cemeteries make marvelous places for strolling, while the Kailua region has freshwater marshes that foster bird-watching opportunities.

NORTH LIGHT IMAGES / GETTY IMAGES ©

☑ **Top Tip**

For more on the City and County of Honolulu's gardens, check out the **Department of Parks and Recreation** at (www.honolulu.gov/parks/hbg.html).

Gardens

Lyon Arboretum A 200-acre arboretum run by the University of Hawai'i. (p63)

Foster Botanical Garden Honolulu's oldest botanical garden dating from the 1850s. (p33)

Koko Crater Botanical Garden Inside dry Koko Crater; spectacular plumeria. (p109)

Ho'omaluhia Botanical Garden Beneath the dramatic cliffs of the Ko'olau Range. (p118)

Sanctuaries

Kawai Nui Marsh Ancient Hawaiian fishpond with paved recreational path. (p118)

Hamakua Marsh Wildlife Sanctuary Nature preserve with habitat for endangered waterbirds. (p118)

Cemeteries

National Memorial Cemetery of the Pacific Better known as the 'Punchbowl,' as atmospheric a cemetery as it gets. (p33)

Valley of the Temples & Byōdō-in Peaceful and park-like with a replica of a 900-year old Japanese temple. (p117)

Best
For Free

A surprising number of sights and activities that you may enjoy on your trip to Honolulu will see you leaving your wallet in your pocket. Beaches are free – Hanauma Bay is a notable exception; hiking trails are free; some city-run botanical gardens are free; and public tennis courts are free, even if you're playing at night under lights!

MICHELE FALZONE / GETTY IMAGES ©

Museums

Hawai'i State Art Museum Art from Hawaii's multiethnic communities at this superb art museum. (p30)

Honolulu Museum of Art at First Hawaiian Center Mixed-media exhibits of modern works at the high-rise First Hawaiian Bank headquarters. (p47)

Hawai'i Army Museum Exhibits on the US military presence in Hawaii; entrance by donation. (p80)

WWII Connections

WWII Valor in the Pacific National Monument Visit the USS Arizona Memorial and monument museums; other Pearl Harbor attractions charge. (p65)

National Memorial Cemetery of the Pacific Admire the thought-provoking Punchbowl and views over Honolulu. (p33)

Historic Buildings

Aloha Tower Sweeping views from this 1926 landmark, once Honolulu's tallest building. (p33)

Moana Surfrider Hotel Take a tour of this iconic Waikiki hotel, opened in 1901. (p79)

Royal Hawaiian Hotel Free tours of Waikiki's historic 'Pink Palace.' (p79)

State Capitol Check out the State Capitol, unique in design among US state capitol buildings. (p30)

☑ **Top Tip**

Don't miss the free **Kuhio Beach Torch Lighting & Hula Show** (p71) in Waikiki.

Gardens & Temples

Koko Crater Botanical Garden Hawaiian flora in dry volcanic crater. (p109)

Ho'omaluhia Botanical Garden O'ahu's largest botanical garden of 400 acres. (p118)

Ulupo Heiau State Monument Imposing platform temple of the ancients not far from Kailua. (p117)

Survival Guide

Survival Guide

Before You Go

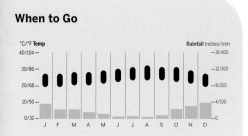

When to Go

°C/°F **Temp**
Rainfall inches/mm

➡ **High Season (mid-Dec–mid-Apr)** High occupancy and prices; book rooms and activities far ahead; rainiest and coolest time of the year.

➡ **Low Season (mid-Apr–May)** Weather still temperate; airfares and lodging rates drop; fewer crowds.

➡ **Shoulder Season (Jun–Aug)** Dry, hot weather; visitor spike due to school summer vacation on mainland; prices up.

➡ **Low Season (Sep–mid-Dec)** Great weather; crowds and prices at their lowest; good airfares.

Book Your Stay

☑ **Top Tip** Remember that 14% in taxes will be added to lodging rates that you see; many hotels and resorts add an 'amenity fee' per day that you are there. Check what is included when booking.

➡ Most of Honolulu's accommodations are in Waikiki.

➡ Advance bookings are highly recommended in high and shoulder seasons.

➡ You will pay more if you are beachfront; smaller hotels inland from the beach may be less than half the price.

➡ The terms 'ocean view' and 'partial ocean view', are used liberally – you may need a periscope to spot the waves. 'City', 'garden' or 'mountain' views may be euphemisms for overlooking the parking lot. Try to check what you're getting.

➡ Overnight parking fees may make a long-term rental car unattractive.

Useful Websites

Lonely Planet (www.lonelyplanet.com) Author-recommendation reviews and online booking.

Vacation Rental by Owner (www.vrbo.com) Rent direct from owners.

Affordable Paradise (www.affordable-paradise.com) Private accommodations in Hawaii.

HomeAway (www.homeaway.com) Vacation rentals.

Captain Cook Resorts (www.captaincookresorts.com) Good vacation options in Waikiki.

Hawaii's Best Bed & Breakfast (www.bestbnb.com) Bed & Breakfasts, private inns and vacation rentals.

Best Budget

Hostelling International (HI) Waikiki (www.hostelsaloha.com) Tidy hostel just a few blocks from the beach.

Hostelling International (HI) Honolulu (www.hostelsaloha.com) Simple hostel up near UH.

Central Branch YMCA (www.ymcahonolulu.org) Basic rooms for unfussy budget travelers at the Y.

Waikiki Beachside Hostel (www.waikikibeachsidehostel.com) A good option at the Kapi'olani Park end of Waikiki.

Royal Grove Hotel (www.royalgrovehotel.com) Candy-pink hotel with lots of returnees.

Waikiki Prince (www.waikikiprince.com) Cheery compact rooms at a good price.

Best Midrange

Aston at the Waikiki Banyan (www.astonwaikikibanyan.com) A good family option a block back from the beach.

Aqua Bamboo (www.aquabamboo.com) Refreshed boutique hotel on Kuhio Ave.

Aqua Aloha Surf Waikiki (www.alohasurfhotelwaikiki.com) Bargain hotel back next to Ala Wai Canal.

Castle Waikiki Grand (www.WaikikiGrandCondos.com) Small

gay-friendly condo hotel opposite the zoo.

Waikiki Parc (www.waikikiparc.com) Hip hotel in the center of the action.

Hotel Renew (www.hotelrenew.com) Design-savvy, eco-friendly hotel half-block from the beach.

Best Top End

Royal Hawaiian (www.royal-hawaiian.com) The 'Pink Palace' was Waikiki's original luxury hotel.

Moana Surfrider (www.moana-surfrider.com) Waikiki's most historic hotel, opened in 1901.

Halekulani (www.halekulani.com) Modern sophistication at this beachfront hotel.

Sheraton Waikiki (www.sheraton-waikiki.com) High-rise waterfront hotel; great for families.

Lotus Honolulu (www.lotushonoluluhotel.com) Hip boutique hotel at Sans Souci beach.

Modern Honolulu (www.themodernhonolulu.com) Ocean-view rooms near Ala Wai Yacht Harbor.

Arriving in Honolulu

Honolulu International Airport

The vast majority of flights into Hawaii land at **Honolulu International Airport** (HNL; ☎808-836-6411; http://hawaii.gov/hnl; 300 Rodgers Blvd, Honolulu), about 6 miles northwest of downtown Honolulu and 9 miles northwest of Waikiki. O'ahu's only commercial airport, it's a hub for domestic, international and inter-island flights.

Bus You can reach downtown Honolulu, Ala Moana Center and Waikiki via TheBus 19 or 20. Buses run every 20 minutes from 6am to 11pm daily; the regular fare is $2.50. Luggage is restricted to what you can hold on your lap or stow under the seat (maximum size 22" x 14" x 9").

Shuttle Roberts Hawaii (☎808-441-7800; www.airportwaikikishuttle.com) operates 24-hour door-to-door shuttle buses to Waikiki's hotels, departing every 20 to 60 minutes. Fares average $12 to $15 one way, or $20 to $30 round trip; surcharges apply for bicycles, surfboards, golf clubs and extra baggage. Reservations are helpful, but not always required for airport pickups. For return trips, reserve at least 48 hours in advance.

Taxi You can reach Waikiki by taxi (average cab fare $35 to $45) in 25 to 45 minutes.

Car The easiest driving route to Waikiki is via the Nimitz Hwy (Hwy 92), which becomes Ala Moana Blvd. For the fast lane, take the H-1 (Lunalilo) Fwy eastbound, then follow signs 'To Waikiki'. The drive between the airport and Waikiki takes 25 to 45 minutes, depending on traffic.

Getting Around

Bicycle

☑ **Best for ...** exploring local neighborhoods.

It's possible to cycle around O'ahu, but consider taking TheBus to get beyond Honolulu metro area traffic. Hawaii's **Department of Transportation** (http://hidot.hawaii.gov/highways/bike-map-oahu) publishes a Bike O'ahu route map, available free online.

Bus

☑ **Best for ...** getting to Ala Moana, Downtown & Chinatown, Pearl Harbor and Hanauma Bay.

➡ O'ahu's public bus system, **TheBus** (☎808-848-5555; www.thebus.org; adult fare $2.50, 4-day visitor pass $35; ⏱infoline 5:30am-10pm), is extensive but most hiking trails and some popular viewpoints are beyond its reach.

➡ Ala Moana Center is Honolulu's central bus transfer point.

➤ Although buses are fast and frequent, you can't set your watch by them. Especially in Waikiki, buses sometimes bottleneck, with one packed bus after another passing right by crowded bus stops.

➤ All buses are wheelchair-accessible and have front-loading racks that accommodate two bicycles at no extra charge – just let the driver know first.

Car, Motorcycle & Moped

☑ **Best for ...** exploring O'ahu.

➤ All major car-rental agencies have rental cars either at Honolulu International Airport or about a mile outside the airport off Nimitz Hwy (airport courtesy shuttles available).

➤ Most major car-rental agencies have multiple branch locations in Waikiki. These branches can be less hassle (and less expensive, given steep overnight parking costs at Waikiki hotels) if you're only renting a car for a day.

Bus Fares & Passes

➤ The one-way adult fare is $2.50 (children aged six to 17 $1.25). Use coins or $1 bills; bus drivers don't give change. One free transfer (two connections) is available from the driver.

➤ A $35 visitor pass valid for unlimited rides over four consecutive days is sold at Waikiki's ubiquitous ABC Stores and **TheBus Pass Office** (☎808-848-4444; www.thebus.org; Kalihi Transit Center, cnr Middle St & Kamehameha Hwy; 🕑7:30am-4pm Mon-Fri).

➤ A monthly bus pass ($60), valid for unlimited rides during a calendar month (not just any 30-day period), is sold at TheBus Pass Office, 7-Eleven convenience stores and Foodland supermarkets.

➤ Seniors (65 years and older) and anyone with a physical disability can buy a $10 discount ID card at TheBus Pass Office entitling them to pay $1 per one-way fare or $5/30 for a pass valid for unlimited rides during one calendar month/year.

➤ In Waikiki, independent car-rental agencies may offer much lower rates, especially for one-day rentals and 4WD vehicles. They're also more likely to rent to drivers under 25. Some also rent mopeds and motorcycles, and a few specialize in smart cars and hybrid vehicles.

➤ Surprisingly, a moped or motorcycle can be more expensive to rent than a car.

Taxi

☑ **Best for ...** late nights and groups sharing the cost.

➤ Taxis have meters and charge $3.10 at flagfall, plus $3.60 per mile and 50¢ per suitcase or backpack.

➤ They're readily available at the airport, resort hotels and shopping centers. Otherwise, you'll probably have to call for one.

Essential Information

Business Hours

☑ **Top Tip** Some shops in Waikiki will be open much later than those in other areas.

Nonstandard hours are listed in reviews; standard business hours are as follows:

Banks 8:30am to 4pm Monday to Friday, some to 6pm Friday and 9am to noon or 1pm Saturday

Bars & clubs To midnight daily, some to 2am Thu-Sat

Businesses 8:30am-4:30pm Mon-Fri; some post offices 9am-noon Sat

Restaurants Breakfast 6-10am, lunch 11:30am-2pm, dinner 5-9:30pm

Shops 9am-5pm Mon-Sat, some also noon-5pm Sun; major shopping centers keep extended hours

Electricity

120V/60Hz

120V/60Hz

Emergencies

Police 📞911
Fire 📞911
Ambulance 📞911

Money

➡ The unit of currency is the US dollar ($) which is divided into 100 cents (¢).

➡ Major banks, such as the **Bank of Hawaii** (www.boh.com) and **First Hawaiian Bank** (www.fhb.com), have extensive ATM networks throughout O'ahu.

➡ Hawaii has a 4.17% state sales tax.

Tipping

For those from countries where tipping is not the norm, tipping is *not* optional in Hawaii; only withhold tips in cases of outrageously bad service. In Hawaii, tipping practices are the same as on the US mainland, roughly:

Airport and hotel porters $2 per bag, minimum of $5 per cart.

Bartenders 15% to 20% per round, minimum of $1 per drink.

Hotel maids $2 to $4 per night, left under the card provided; more if you're messy.

Parking valets At least $2 when your keys are returned.

Restaurant servers 15% to 20%, unless a service charge is already on the bill.

Taxi drivers 15% of the metered fare, rounded up to the next dollar.

Public Holidays

On the following holidays, banks, schools and government offices (including post offices) close, and transportation and museums operate on a Sunday schedule. Holidays falling on a weekend are usually observed the following Monday.

New Year's Day January 1

Martin Luther King Jr Day Third Monday in January

Presidents' Day Third Monday in February

Easter March or April

Prince Kuhio Day March 26

Memorial Day Last Monday in May

King Kamehameha Day June 11

Independence Day July 4

Statehood Day Third Friday in August

Labor Day First Monday in September

Columbus Day Second Monday in October

Veterans Day November 11

Thanksgiving Fourth Thursday in November

Christmas Day December 25

Safe Travel

In general, Hawaii is a safe place to visit. The **Visitor Aloha Society of Hawaii** (VASH; www.visitoralohasocietyofhawaii.org) provides nonmonetary emergency aid to short-stay visitors who become the victims of accidents or crimes.

☑ **Top Tip** Try not to leave anything of value in your car anytime you walk away from it. If you must, pack things well out of sight before pulling up to park.

Theft & Violence

➡ O'ahu is notorious for thefts from parked cars, both locals' and tourist rentals.

➡ Stay attuned to the vibe on any beaches at night, even in Waikiki.

Tsunami

➡ The tsunami warning system is tested on the first working day of every month at 11:45am for less than one minute. If you hear a tsunami warning siren at any other time, head for higher ground immediately.

Telephone

Mobile Phones

➡ Among US providers, Verizon has the most extensive network.

➡ International travelers need a multiband GSM phone in order to make calls in the USA.

➡ With an unlocked multiband phone, using a US prepaid rechargeable SIM card is usually cheaper than using your own network.

➡ SIM cards are available at any major telecommunications or electronics store.

Dialing Codes

➡ All Hawaii phone numbers consist of a three-digit area code (☎808) followed by a seven-digit local number.

➡ To call long-distance from one Hawaiian island to another, dial ☎1-808 + local number.

➡ Always dial 📞1 before toll-free numbers (800, 888 etc).

➡ To call Canada from Hawaii, dial 📞1 + area code + local number (international rates apply).

➡ For all other international calls, dial 📞011 + country code + area code + local number.

➡ Local directory assistance 📞411

➡ Long-distance directory assistance 📞1- (area code) -555-1212

➡ Toll-free directory assistance 📞1-800-555-1212

➡ Operator 📞0

Tourist Information

➡ In the arrivals area at the airport there are tourist information desks with helpful staff.

➡ Honolulu produces stacks of tourist brochures and magazines, which are packed with discount coupons, such as:

101 Things to Do (www.101thingstodo.com)

This Week (http://this weekmagazines.com)

Spotlight on O'ahu (www. spotlighthawaii.com)

➡ For pre-trip planning, browse the information-packed website of the **Hawaii Visitors & Convention Bureau** (www. gohawaii.com).

Travelers with Disabilities

➡ Bigger, newer hotels and resorts in Hawaii have elevators, TDD-capable phones and wheelchair-accessible rooms (reserve these well in advance).

➡ Traffic intersections have dropped curbs and audible crossing signals in cities and some towns, as well as all along Waikiki's beachfront.

➡ **Honolulu's Department of Parks and Recreation** (www. honolulu.gov/parks/ dprbeachaccess.html) provides all-terrain beach mats and wheelchairs for free (call ahead to make arrangements) at several beaches, including Ala Moana, Hanauma Bay and Sans Souci.

➡ All **public buses** on O'ahu are wheelchair-accessible and will 'kneel' if you're unable to use the steps – just let the driver know that you need the lift or ramp.

➡ **Access Aloha Travel** (www.accessalohatravel. com) is a local travel agency that can help book wheelchair-accessible accommodations, rental vans and sightseeing tours.

➡ **Disability & Communication Access Board** (www.hawaii.gov/health/ dcab/travel) offers online 'Traveler Tips' about airports, accessible transportation, sightseeing, and medical and other support services.

Visas

➡ Under the US **Visa Waiver Program** (VWP), visas are not required for citizens of 38 countries for stays of up to 90 days.

➡ Under the VWP you must have a return ticket (or onward ticket to any foreign destination) that is nonrefundable in the USA.

➡ All VWP travelers must register online at least 72 hours before arrival with the **Electronic System for Travel Authorization** (https://esta.cbp.dhs. gov/esta/). Registration is valid for two years.

➡ Travelers who don't qualify for the VWP must apply for a tourist visa. The process involves a personal interview and can take several weeks, so apply early.

Behind the Scenes

Send Us Your Feedback

We love to hear from travelers – your comments help make our books better. We read every word, and we guarantee that your feedback goes straight to the authors. Visit **lonelyplanet.com/contact** to submit your updates and suggestions.

Note: We may edit, reproduce and incorporate your comments in Lonely Planet products such as guidebooks, websites and digital products, so let us know if you don't want your comments reproduced or your name acknowledged. For a copy of our privacy policy visit lonelyplanet.com/privacy.

Craig's Thanks

A huge thanks to my on-the-road assistant and exceptionally beautiful wife, Yuriko! And cheers to Paul & Nezia, Phil & Liwei, and everyone else who helped us out.

Acknowledgments

Cover photograph: Waikiki Beach, Honolulu, Michele Falzone/AWL ©

This Book

This 1st edition of Lonely Planet's *Pocket Honolulu* was researched and written by Craig McLachlan. This guidebook was produced by the following:

Destination Editor Alexander Howard **Product Editors** Elin Berglund, Elizabeth Jones **Senior Cartographers** Valentina Kremenchutskaya, Anthony Phelan **Book Designer** Jennifer Mullins

Assisting Editors Judith Bamber, Jodie Martire **Cover Researcher** Naomi Parker **Thanks to** Sasha Baskett, Kate Chapman, Ryan Evans, Kate Mathews, Claire Naylor, Diana Saengkham, Lyahna Spencer, Tony Wheeler, Tracy Whitmey

Index

See also separate subindexes for:

⊗ **Eating p156**

🍷 **Drinking p157**

⭐ **Entertainment p157**

🔒 **Shopping p157**

➕ **Sports & Activities p158**

Our Writer

Craig McLachlan

A Kiwi from the southern end of the Polynesian triangle, Craig is a regular in Honolulu and has an MBA from the University of Hawai'i at Manoa. He loves nothing more than hanging out at Waimanalo Beach, eating *poke* and bodyboarding. Other Lonely Planet guidebooks he has worked on include *Greek Islands*, *Japan* and *Rarotonga, Samoa & Tonga*. Craig considers himself a 'freelance anything' and past jobs have included pilot, karate instructor, tour leader, hiking guide and Japanese interpreter. Five books have been published about his various adventures – he once set the record for climbing Japan's 100 Famous Mountains!

For more on what Craig is up to, see www.craig mclachlan.com.

Published by Lonely Planet Publications Pty Ltd
ABN 36 005 607 983
1st edition – Sep 2015
ISBN 978 1 74360 516 5
© Lonely Planet 2015   Photographs © as indicated 2015
10 9 8 7 6 5 4 3 2 1
Printed in China